est

est*

60 Hours That Transform Your Life

ADELAIDE BRY

Harper & Row, Publishers

New York, Hagerstown, San Francisco, London

* Erhard Seminars Training

To my parents and their parents who
were still concerned with most of the
three feet, and to my children, Barbara
and Douglas, and to their children, who
will be able to experience that last
quarter inch

Grateful acknowledgment is made for permission to reprint the following:

Excerpts from *East West Journal* interview with Werner Erhard reprinted by permission of *East West Journal*.

Lyrics from "Looking for Space" by John Denver reprinted by permission of Cherry Lane Music Co. Copyright 1975 Cherry Lane Music Co. (ASCAP). All rights reserved.

"Adelaide Bry did a great job. The book is readable, accurate and gives a balanced view of est. Adelaide has demonstrated her integrity as a writer by extensive research, verifying the quotes she uses, checking and rechecking her facts, and by stating her opinion as opinion rather than as fact. I support the author."

—Werner Erhard

Acknowledgments

Marjorie Bair and Herb Hamsher, you are both fabulous. Your assistance with this book was beautiful. Thank you. I love you.

In New York and California and points in between, I send my love to all the est graduates who shared their experience of est with me; and especially to Lea, Christian, Rick, Cathy, Morgan, Fred, Lee, Nessa, Bill, Ted, John, Jim, Bob, Alfred, Brad, Phyllis, Stephen, Judy, Carol, Michael, and Brunhilde. Thank you.

Thanks to Dr. Edward Blair Guy for my official introduction to the Federal Correctional Institution at Lompoc.

Thank you, Werner, for creating est, and thank you, est and Morty Lefkoe, for assisting me in getting the facts.

To Alice Kenner and Nancy Cone, of Harper & Row, thanks for editorial excellence and grace under pressure.

Contents

Cheese

"Obviously the truth is what's so. Not so obviously, it's also so what."

—Werner Erhard

If you put a rat in front of a bunch of tunnels and put cheese in one of them, the rat will go up and down the tunnels looking for the cheese. If every time you do the experiment you put the cheese down the fourth tunnel, eventually you'll get a successful rat. This rat knows the right tunnel and goes directly to it every time.

If you now move the cheese out of the fourth tunnel and put it at the end of another tunnel, the rat still goes down the fourth tunnel. And, of course, gets no cheese. He then comes out of the tunnel, looks the tunnels over, and goes right back down the cheeseless fourth tunnel. Unrewarded, he comes out of the tunnel, looks the tunnels over again, goes back down the fourth tunnel again, and again finds no cheese.

Now the difference between a rat and a human being is that eventually the rat will stop going down the fourth tunnel and will look down the other tunnels, and a human being will go down the tunnel with no cheese forever. Rats, you see, are only interested in cheese. But human beings care more about going down the right tunnel.

It is belief which allows human beings to go down the fourth tunnel *ad nauseam*. They go on doing what they do without any real satisfaction, without any nurturing, because they come to believe that what they are doing is *right*. And they will do this forever, even if there is no cheese in the tunnel, as long as they believe in it and can prove that they are in the right tunnel.

People who are getting satisfaction out of life don't have

to prove they are in the right tunnel. Therefore they don't need beliefs.

Belief is all you have when you're not getting satisfaction in your life.

This Werner Erhard story, familiar to most est graduates, is an introduction to a simple but basic notion—that one's beliefs about reality may have no relationship to what is really happening.

Get it?

1

How's Your Life?

"Man keeps looking for a truth that fits his reality. Given our reality, the truth doesn't fit."
—Werner Erhard

How is your life working right this minute? Do you *believe* that it would be better if you had more money? A different spouse or lover? Bigger and better orgasms? More respect, or responsibility, or income? Would it be better if you had better looks, brains, figure? If you were better liked? Or if, as a child, you had received more love, kindness, education, or opportunity?

Undoubtedly you can answer "yes" to at least one of the above. How nice, then, to know that Werner Erhard has said, "I happen to think that you are perfect exactly the way you are." He goes on to say, "The problem is that people get stuck acting the way they were, instead of being the way they are." So if it's "getting better" that you're after, you're stuck in a belief about "getting better." Getting better, however, is not what est is about.

If est isn't interested in changing people, what does it do? What is this process that has so far trained 75,000 men, women and children and whose founder and leader has stated that he intends to train forty million?

From one point of view, est can be seen as beginning where everything else leaves off.

Starting with Freud, and followed in short order by other systems that were variations on Freudian themes, contemporary Americans have become accustomed to the notion that they can talk, reason, or scream their way out of problems or neuroses and into sanity, or wholeness.

After World War II, psychoanalysis became the change agent for those who could afford it. But that method of getting in touch with childhood experiences and of eradicating or accepting whatever mother, father, and environment had "done to" us is extremely costly and often doesn't work. Understanding one's past doesn't necessarily lead to change. And often, screaming doesn't either.

est clearly states in its general information brochure that "it is not like group therapy, sensitivity training, encounter groups, positive thinking, meditation, hypnosis, mind control, behavior modification, or psychology. In fact," the statement concludes, "est is not therapy and is not psychology."

Implicit in these words is the premise that what they're offering is something quite different. It was a search for something I was not yet able to define—something beyond the psychologies, something "quite different"—that led me to est.

I first learned of est through a young friend who called excitedly from California to tell me about it. She was certain that I'd be interested in what she described as "this latest head/body trip" because of what she knew about my other involvements.

In addition to being a practicing psychotherapist and a writer, I am a seeker of truth, self-realization, and spiritual and physical highs. You name it in terms of self-improvement discipline, and chances are I've done it. I've studied yoga and transcendental meditation. I've been Rolfed and psychoanalyzed. I've "done" nude marathons, encounter groups, transactional analysis, Gestalt, guided LSD trips, and Silva Mind Control. Most recently, prior to est training, I went through the heady forty-day Arica training.

I had experienced much of the growth (sometimes called "grope") movement of the sixties, had undergone some important changes, but was still hungry for more.

In my quest for growth, for meaning, for inner change, I was but one of many searching for surcease from the malaise that increasingly has marked middle-class America since World War II. I, like many others, was searching for *satisfaction*.

The affluence that had been so ambitiously pursued through the sixties in this country, and to a great extent attained, clearly wasn't living up to its promise: happiness ever after. As more and more of us bought ourselves swimming pools, foreign vacations, and early retirements both the divorce rate and crime rate soared.

Two cars in a suburban garage didn't seem to change our feelings of loneliness, alienation, disappointment, or despair. Nor did the divorce or affair that often followed, because they were responses to symptoms rather than to causes.

Another sacred cow, education—and especially college education—also turned out to promise more than it delivered. The expectation was that the young, their heads crammed with information, would emerge from school equipped to create better or happier lives than their parents had. The fact was that a lot of these youngsters rejected their parents' work and moral ethics, creating still further alienation.

Along with money, education, and status, the sacrosanctity of the family also began to be questioned. As the extended family became a thing of the past, and nuclear families experienced increasing isolation in their suburban homes and urban apartments, the task of rearing the children fell almost completely to the woman parent. This proved an incredibly heavy burden for both mother and children, and they suffered and suffocated in it, while fathers grew more remote.

Cornell University social psychologist Urie Bronfenbrenner noted in a *Newsweek* cover story on the contemporary family that the incidence of family pathology is spreading swiftly among all sectors of U.S. society. "The middle-class family," he said, ". . . is approaching the level of social disorganization that characterized the low income family of the early 1960's."*

According to the same article, teen-age drug abuse and alcoholism are also on the rise. Suicide has become the second lead-

* September 22, 1975.

ing cause of death among young Americans between the ages of fifteen and twenty-four, and the rate of juvenile delinquency is increasing at such a pace that today one child in nine can be expected to appear in juvenile court before the age of eighteen.

To chronicle the ills of the past couple of decades, by way of understanding how we got to est, is not my purpose here. Suffice it to note, at the risk of sounding simplistic, that our values are breaking down in all areas—relationships, education, economics, politics, etc.—and that out of this crisis new alternatives are being sought.

Many of us have become, like myself, seekers of a better way —a way out of the confusion, the complexities, the uncertainties that seem greater now than ever before.

This search is reflected in such items as the fact that every suburban community has its yoga class; in the incredible sales figures of books on mediums (Edgar Cayce), magicians (Don Juan), and mystics (Sri Aurobindo, Chogyam Trumpa Rinpoche); in the fact that whole families take the phone off the hook before dinner for twenty minutes of transcendental meditation (at last count more than 450,000 people have studied TM); and in the consciousness expansion still sought through such hallucinogenic drugs as LSD and mescaline.

A friend of mine, married to a longshoreman, is studying Tai Chi and is heavily into its philosophy. A businessman I know is using biofeedback to reduce his blood pressure. And a woman with whom I once pushed baby carriages leaves a luncheon early to meet with her Zen master. It's no longer unusual to encounter people who have left careers they sweated for, because the work or the goals were no longer "meaningful." I did it—as have a half a dozen friends in their middle years.

These reports of individual experiences are not isolated ones. They have become part of a spontaneous movement called the "consciousness revolution." The movement is taking many forms, going in many directions, and has many spokesmen. Many see it as the beginning of the New Age, a time in mankind's evolution which has been prophesied for centuries and which is both an end and a beginning; a critical point in history in which man and his planet are undergoing vast transformation.

This new consciousness, essentially an experience of self, ranges from a new experience of one's body to a new experience of God—which is not, as it may appear, contradictory. When *Time* magazine in a 1969 cover story proclaimed that God was dead, it was talking about the all-powerful Judeo-Christian God, who might zap us (that is, send us to hell) if we didn't behave ourselves. It was a God beyond us, a Father whose love was conditional.

The God of the seventies is out of the Eastern tradition. It is God within, and thus God and the self are inseparable. One can experience God directly, and thousands are doing just that daily through such consciousness-altering techniques as meditation and chanting.

William Irwin Thompson, in his brilliant exploration of the new planetary culture, *Passages About Earth,* writes, "A new ideology is being created . . . Perhaps it will take no institutional form at all, for it now seems that social institutions are no longer adequate vehicles of cultural evolution. We cannot go to church to find radiant Godhead, to the army to find glory in war, or to the universities to find aesthetic transfiguration or wisdom. Now only mysticism seems well suited to the postinstitutional anarchism of technetronic culture, on the one hand, and the infinite posthuman universe on the other."*

And Marshall McLuhan, in a *Playboy* interview (March, 1969), speaks of the imminence of "the universality of consciousness foreseen by Dante when he predicted that men would continue as no more than broken fragments until they were unified into an inclusive consciousness." This new consciousness, he says, is now possible with the development of the electronic media.

If cosmic consciousness is the goal, then inner experience is the means. Futurists such as Thompson and McLuhan are talking about the mystic intuitive experience. Others are focusing

* New York: Harper & Row, 1974.

on the feeling experience. (Note that no one is talking about the intellectual experience, which is becoming as passé as psychoanalysis.)

Part of how you feel is how your body feels, which of course is directly related to how your feelings feel. Wilhelm Reich's theories of character armor (body defenses against feelings) and the flow of energy within the body foreshadowed the current Western interest in such systems as bioenergetics, the Alexander technique, Rolfing, Hatha Yoga, and Shiatsu. All these techniques seek to liberate the body and focus on inner well-being as opposed to outer success.

Esalen, the number one growth center of the sixties, is now concentrating on increasing body energy toward flowing with the universe. Among their "new" techniques: tennis and golf!

Those deeply into body techniques claim that the story of our lives is stored in aching muscles, low back pains, headaches, and all the other aches we try to eliminate with tranquilizers, sedatives, and painkillers, drowning our feelings in order to "feel better."

In accepting the fact that body feelings are inseparable from emotional feelings, the question "How do you feel?" becomes more relevant today than ever.

When I was a child, I wouldn't dream of telling people what I felt unless it was an "up" feeling, nor would I divulge my feelings about another person unless they were positive. But it was O.K. to describe the bellyaches and headaches that resulted from the fear or anger or other taboo emotions I couldn't talk about.

Nowadays people express their feelings about rage, sex, sorrow—you name it—with the ease that their parents once talked about the weather. Which may be one of the factors that led Jean-Paul Sartre, in a recent interview, to predict a future "transparent man" in whom a thought would be immediately visible, eliminating the need or desire to hide it or pretend another.

The keynote of the present is in the words "unity" and "integration." Thus, the new disciplines seek to integrate mind, body, and soul—how we sit, the way we breathe, what we eat, what our inner voices tell us, how our gut reacts, who we really are—so that we can *experience* our totality, our wholeness, our oneness with the universe.

A lot of this may not sound especially new and, in fact, a lot of it isn't. What *is* new is the *way* it is becoming known. In Arica,* I went through meditations and special exercises to experience my oneness with all living things and my harmony with the vast universe. In the past, the closest I might have come to this understanding was by listening to someone pontificate from a pulpit or lectern on the ways of God.

Which gets me back to est. If what you have, what you do, what you think you are supposed to be, isn't working very well; if hard work, success, romantic love and all the other concepts you were taught were important as a child no longer seem to have meaning in your life; then maybe it's time to look elsewhere, away from the tenets of your past into the here and now of your experience. One way to describe what est is all about is to say it's into the here and now of experienced experience.

In experiencing your own nature in the est training, the est literature states, you are able to transform your ability to experience life. More specifically, the training offers an opportunity to realize a transformation of your experience of knowing; of your experience of experiencing; of your experience of self; of your experience of others.

Werner Erhard, est's founder, described the training in an interview in *East West Journal* (September, 1974) in a characteristically est-ian manner (some call it "mind-fucking"; others, who feel explanations are irrelevant, say that it doesn't really matter *what* Werner says, it's how he says it; and still others think his style is dynamite and emulate it all the time).

In answer to the *Journal*'s question, "What is est?" Werner said, "est is a sixty-hour experience which opens an additional

* A self-transformation discipline developed by Oscar Ichazo, in Chile, to improve clarity of mind and body through a forty-day curriculum of exercise and movement for the physical body, and meditation, mantram, and individual analysis for spiritual and cognitive growth.

dimension of living to your awareness. The training is designed to transform the level at which you experience life so that living becomes a process of expanding satisfaction.

"Another part of the answer is there is no 'answer.' est actually is an experience. But if you go around telling people that, you won't have anything to talk about and you need something to say about it. It is a very individual experience. And because of that, it's something that is created *by* the individual. In other words, est is not created by the trainer or the group that the person goes to train with, it's an experience—like all experiences —which is created by the individual who is experiencing the experience. . . . My notion is that what happens in the training is that the individual is given an opportunity to create original experiences, or to *re*-create original experiences—experiences which that individual originally created. . . .

"It's definitely a way past the mind. It transcends the mind. Actually, what I would really say—because I think it communicates better than anything, although it is not totally accurate—is that it *blows the mind*."*

A friend of mine put it another way: "What you get out of est is that you stop being an asshole groveling in your shit and you start finding out what being *alive* is all about."

How's *your* life?

* My italics.

Gerry and Marcia*

Gerry, thirty, is a real estate salesman. He is quick and friendly and immediately makes people he's with comfortable. Marcia, his wife, is an executive secretary and appears serious and gentle.

GERRY: Our real estate office is like a branch of est. My uncle, who owns the business, is a graduate and everyone else had taken the training except me. I felt pressured to do est. I didn't want to and, at the same time I also did.

Yeah, it worked. While the real estate business isn't great now, so I can't claim dollars and cents results, I know I'm more confident and aware in dealing with people. I can look them in the eye, literally and figuratively.

Probably the main thing that's resulted from the training is that I've thrown away my Bufferin. For years I had almost daily headaches from tension. They're almost all gone. When I get one now, I don't fight it. I just experience it. I've always had physical ailments. Last year it was simulated heart attacks and pains in my arms and chest, which scared the hell out of me. In college I used to get tonsillitis. I was always sick with something. I was constantly abusing myself.

In the training I saw how I was never happy about anything. Just like my Dad. He gets to feel like a total failure because some other guy has a better car or house or bigger business. But I now see what a racket that is.

* This and the other autobiographies of est graduates throughout the book are representative of the many interviews I conducted. I have changed most of the subjects' names, at their request. There are no strongly negative statements simply because I was unable to find any. Just before this book went to press I finally met a woman who felt the training was useless, although not destructive. "I don't feel saved, I don't feel not saved, I don't feel much of anything after est," she told me. "My life was pretty much O.K. the way it was and it's O.K. now." That was it!

My brother-in-law, an orthopedic surgeon, took the training. He went into it skeptical and came out of it really impressed. Now he tells a lot of his patients, "If you want to get rid of your lower-back pain go to est. If you want to hold on to it, you can do that too." It might just ruin his business.

MARCIA: After Gerry took it, I felt out of it. Everyone bugged me to take the training. I'm an optimist. I didn't think I needed it. I finally did the training and found it really good.

Gerry's and my main hang-up was whether or not we should have children. I didn't want them—not yet, anyway. Otherwise our relationship had been pretty good.

Now we feel we want to have children eventually. And it is all right not to have them now; we don't *have* to have kids because our friends do. Now I feel more confident about taking care of a child.

Some mornings when I feel that I want to leave my job, or just not bother to show up, Gerry and I talk and I see that I have a choice. And I get there.

We both see, now, how a lot of people cover up what goes on with them. We also see our needs and desires. Having a house and kids is no longer "it."

I'm more involved and aware of myself. That's what life is all about.

2

In the Beginning

QUESTION: *Has est changed your life?*
ANSWER: *Yes. Now I carry all my troubles around with me instead of just some of them.*

Around New York the est training is called the "no piss training." At the time I was considering taking it, bathroom breaks were up to seven hours apart.*

I very much wanted to take the training—I had heard strange and wonderful things about it—but I was hung up on the bathroom thing. The more curious I became, the more I feared I wouldn't be able to maintain control for such a long time.

I blamed this fear on a childhood incident which still haunted me. In the second grade, during a spelling test, my teacher chose to ignore my raised hand signaling that I needed to go to the bathroom. The inevitable happened; I wet my pants. I was so ashamed of this incident that I had never mentioned it to anyone. Now, decades later, I was afraid it would be repeated.

I finally decided to take the training anyway. The decision made, I embarked on the est adventure, a trip that a year later isn't yet over and probably never will be. It now appears to be one of the most valuable experiences I've ever had.

It wasn't until I was well into the training, incidentally, that I *got* what my fear had really been about. I had always avoided situations in which I felt my freedom would be circumscribed; I cherished my independence too much to allow anyone to tell me what to do. A dozen years earlier I had walked out on a fabu-

* They're now down to about four hours.

lous job as the only woman account executive in a large advertising agency just because, regardless of how long, hard, and
creatively I worked, all account executives had to sign in every
morning at 9:00. It wasn't until I went through the training that
I really experienced this as a pattern of my life.

est has two meanings. It is the Latin word for "it is." It is
also an acronym whose initials stand for Erhard Seminars
Training, named after its creator, Werner Erhard. It is always
written in the modest lower case, simple and unostentatious, in
quiet good taste. In contrast to its typographical style, est is an
ebullient, dynamic, expanding operation.

I heard that the people who were taking the training were
not the type of seekers I was used to meeting in the various
therapy/encounter/mind-expansion experiences I had had
over the past dozen years. A good proportion had never been in
therapy and/or been involved in a growth group.

They were young and old, confused and confident, divorced,
married, professionals, housewives, students, rich, not-so-rich
(but rarely poor). The reason they were all flocking to est? Because, even though most of them were doing well, their lives
weren't really satisfying; in est talk, *trying* to make their lives
satisfying wasn't satisfying either.

Almost without exception, they had come to est because
someone they knew had been through it, had raved about it,
and had become living proof that it "worked." A few had read
one of several provocative magazine articles about est. Many
were aware that some famous entertainers were among its graduates: John Denver had written songs praising est; Valerie
Harper had thanked Werner on TV; and Yoko Ono, George
Maharis, Polly Bergen, Joanne Woodward, Cloris Leachman,
Jerry Rubin, and Roy Scheider, as well as four of the Fifth Dimension, were also said to be alumni. (est keeps the names of
its graduates confidential; many graduates, however, speak publicly about their participation in est.)

Clearly, est was enjoying a smashing success. Wherever I
went in New York and San Francisco, I heard remarkable stories from graduates who were effortlessly changing their lives:

making decisions to leave or remain in marriages, resuming relationships with aging parents they had avoided for years, getting out of ruts, getting into better jobs and better relationships, losing weight without trying—continually affirming how much better they were feeling about money, sex, and/or God.

At the same time, a lot of people, weary of the proliferation of all the mind-expanding movements of the last fifteen years, were dismissing est as just one more in a long string of self-helps. The others didn't work for them, and they doubted that est could either.

However, for the same reasons that thousands of others were being drawn to est, I was also curious about it. In addition to the personal benefits that seemed likely, I had a professional interest in finding out what the est game was all about. As a psychotherapist who encountered among my patients many of the problems that people were being "cured" of through est, I wanted to know how the difficult task of changing human beings was being accomplished so quickly and, apparently, so effectively. If est was really doing what everyone said it was doing, and doing it in a span of sixty hours, then it was accomplishing what no person and no one system in Western psychology had yet been able to do. After the training, I saw that est is not "change" but transformation, and emphasizes accepting yourself as you really are.

I was awed by the notion that a simple, quick, relatively inexpensive system (my own psychoanalysis had cost more than $15,000) could help vast numbers of people to transform their lives. I was further impressed with the fact that two professional colleagues of mine were sending their patients to est, claiming that it speeded up the therapy process. In fact, est asks on its application form if the applicant is currently in treatment and, if so, if he's "winning" or "losing" in therapy. If he feels he's losing (that the therapy isn't working), est recommends that he doesn't take the training. In any event, est requires people to inform their therapist.

Despite its glowing references, I still embarked on my est experience behind a mask of skepticism.

Just before I began the training a friend chided me about this latest in a long string of self-improvement ventures. He confided that my forays had become a joke to our mutual friends. I was hurt and angered by what he told me. But then my memory flashed to myself as a young girl—self-assured on the outside, miserable on the inside, split for so many years by torment—and I knew that the only reason I was still alive was that I had refused to capitulate to the terror, pain, and confusion that had ruled much of my life. I would continue my search.

I would take the training. But I would reserve judgment—and attempt to maintain a journalist's detachment.

The adventure began one rainy March evening in New York, where I attended my first est guest seminar, held in a large commercial hotel. (I subsequently attended other guest seminars to take additional notes for this book. The description that follows is a composite of those experiences.) I was barely through the revolving doors when I met my first est representative. She wore an est badge and what looked to me like the vacant, mindless smile I had come to associate with Hare-Krishna-type spiritual disciples. Good God, I thought, what inanities am I getting into this time? In spite of myself, I followed her directions to the seminar, assisted along the short route by other smiling volunteers.

A more prosaic setting for enlightenment would be hard to find. In one of those anonymous hotel ballrooms usually rented for testimonial dinners and political fund-raisers, I joined some 2,000 others, who all looked surprisingly familiar. They were the kind of people I might run into in my local supermarket, or have to dinner, or take an adult-education class with. The majority looked overwhelmingly straight, as if they had just come from an office or a kitchen, leaving behind a sheepskin in the attic and a couple of cars in the garage.

Many of them had come to the guest seminar at the behest of a friend who had graduated; graduates are encouraged (actually, urged) to bring friends, relatives, and acquaintances to these events. (An est mailer I received recently says, in part, "When people choose to take the training, they do so out of their experience of you. Who you are and where you come from inspires people." This is followed by a pitch "to share a Special Guest Seminar with your friends.")

Waiting for the seminar to begin, I perused a booklet describing the est training. It began with a statement of purpose: ". . . to transform your ability to experience living so that the situations you have been trying to change or have been putting up with clear up just in the process of life itself."

I especially connected with the word "trying"; it had characterized my life. I had been *trying* to get rid of a despised temper, *trying* to get out or stay out of depressions, *trying* to be a single parent raising my children with love and wisdom, and *trying* to get thin or stay thin, depending on the year. At this point, not needing to try seemed beautiful—but impossible.

I eavesdropped on conversations around me, listening for hope, anxiety, expectations, annoyance. They were all there.

One woman told another that, after est, a long-married couple they both knew were talking for the first time in years.

An elderly man confessed that his nephew had sent him. "He said my kids might even come to see me once in a while. They live in New York but they hate to visit us. That was enough. That's why I'm here."

From another direction, I heard someone say that he was tired of hating himself. "I've spent thirty years doing it and it's time to stop."

Familiar refrains, I thought. Equally familiar was the fact that, like most Americans, they were looking for solutions in quick cures. Aspirin, ten-day diets, speed-reading, courses that promise short-cuts to success—and now enlightenment in two weekends.

I felt irritable, put-upon, unreceptive. My tape recorder had been temporarily confiscated at the door. I thought that the confiscators were being arbitrary and authoritarian. I was assured that there was a good reason for it, but I suspected paranoia behind the soap-opera smiles. I dug into my handbag for notebook and pen, sorry I had come, anxious to get it over with.

The room quieted when the seminar leaders arrived. Wearing the by-now-familiar beatific smiles, Stewart Esposito and Marcia Martin introduced themselves. They were young and attractive, as were almost all the est volunteers and staff I was to meet.

Marcia began. "The purpose of the training is to transform your ability to experience. We have found the result of that transformed way of experiencing is an expanded experience of aliveness. Our definition of aliveness at est is love, health, happiness, and full self-expression." I had no quarrel with that. I settled in for a sermon, giving only part of my attention to the toothsome twosome.

Before long they had my complete attention. Quickly moving from the general to the particular, they took turns describing their experiences and the est experience. If it was less than high drama, it was nevertheless interesting.

Stewart, like Werner, was formerly a management consultant. He had decided to take the training reluctantly. His justification was that he could take what he learned from it to create his own training system. Despite his initial attitude, he began to see changes in his life after attending just a guest seminar.

Before est, he told us, his business ran him. After est, the reverse was true. He had also lost forty pounds and improved his relationship with his kids.

"When I went to high school," he told us, "I thought I would be happy when I graduated. Then I thought I would be happy after college. Then I thought I would be happy after I got a really good job. I was always 'one day in the future.' Meanwhile, the nourishment, the completeness, of life was missing. I was always waiting for one more thing to make me happy."

For a long time, the "one more thing" was love, Stewart confessed. He then launched into a skit he called the rituals of love. The audience tittered when he was a minute or so into it; it sounded familiar. By the time he hit the finale, they were into a full chortle. I wondered how many of them realized that the joke was on them. His tale went something like this:

"We all need someone to love and someone to love us," he said. "So we behave in such a way that we finally get someone to say 'I love you.' That feels great. It fills our need, but it isn't enough because it is only a symbol of the experience—and the experience is really what we are after. And when it isn't enough, we know what the solution is. The solution is always more. More symbols.

"So then we act in a way that gets them to say again, 'I love you.' But soon that is not enough either and again we know what the solution is. The solution is *more*.

"So we say, you tell me you love me but you don't act like it. And finally when we get them to act like it *that* is not enough either. We figure we have the wrong person and we get somebody else and go through the whole series again.

"You see that, while it is true that you and I need someone to love and someone to love us, gratifying a need does not produce satisfaction. It does not make us feel whole and complete. Where love is concerned, it is only the experience of loving and being loved that is satisfying, and that allows us to be whole and complete.

"The purpose of the training," he explained, "is to allow you to experience that part of you that experiences satisfaction so that whether the symbols 'I love you' are there or not, the experience of being loved, and loving, is. The training allows people an opportunity to come from satisfaction, rather than trying to get to it."

Marcia moved center stage to bring Stewart's words back to the experiential. "I want to share with you one of the biggest expansions in my life," she announced softly. The room became silent as she lowered her voice to a stage whisper. "I was able to let go of needing someone." Her words hung in the air. "I found out I can be happy," she explained, "if I never see 'him' again. I am the source of my own happiness."

It was now Marcia's turn to share what she "got" from est. Among other things, before she took the training, she had been "in love with loving" a man. She wanted him to do the training with her, but he felt that aliveness should be given free in San

Francisco's Golden Gate Park. She talked about it constantly and still he wouldn't go with her. Finally she stopped insisting, at which point he decided that he *would* like to do the training. "We still fight," she shared, "but we fight responsibly now. And," she added, "my relationship with my mother works too."

At a later guest seminar, I heard seminar leader Monique's story. Although she was happy before est (I heard none of the est leaders admit to ever having been unhappy), after the training she was able to let her straightened blond hair go naturally curly; she got a substantial raise (unsolicited) in her airline job; and she was now able to communicate to large groups of people, something she could never do before.

Entertained and warmed-up by these stories of happy transformations, the audience was then ready for the nitty-gritty of est.

The cost of an est training is $250 (up $50 from a year ago). In answer to questions about why the fee is so high, the answer was simply "That's what it costs." In return for this sum, payable in advance, a trainee meets with about 249 other trainees in a hotel ballroom for approximately sixty hours of training over two consecutive weekends. Yes, the guests were told, it's true that you may not go to the bathroom or smoke or eat until the trainer says so. No, you don't have to do anything in the training that you don't choose to.

The question remained: What, exactly, *is* the training? And how does it work? In answer, Stewart gave a brief rundown about belief systems (see Chapter 3) and a general, day-by-day agenda. Like most of the audience, I still didn't know what it was all about by the time the seminar was over. I consoled myself with material from one of the est brochures:

Having someone tell you what it is like to parachute out of an airplane is not the same as experiencing jumping out of an airplane yourself. est is a uniquely personal experience. And, as such, it has meaning only to the person who is experiencing it. After you take the training, you probably won't know *how* it works, you will only know *that* it works.

I was able to accept this *after* the training. For the moment, I dutifully noted what Stewart was saying and tried to accept that it was relevant, and that it was as much information as I was going to get.

The main things that happen the first two days, he told us, are experiencing data (undefined) presented by the trainer, sharing experiences with other trainees (he told us we didn't have to share if we didn't want to), and undergoing processes. He implied that the processes are central to the training but that he couldn't really describe them to us. They happen with your eyes closed, he said, so that you're alone with yourself to look at the way you put your life together. He stressed that it is not meditation. However, other people have described it as resembling "guided meditation." A similar technique is called "guided fantasy." An est brochure gives the following technical definition of a process: "A training process is a method by which a person experiences and looks at, in an expanded state of consciousness and without judgment, what is actually so with regard to specific areas in his or her life, and one's fixed or unconscious attitudes about those areas. The intended result of doing a training process is a release to greater spontaneity."

Between his talk and answers to questions from the audience, I began to piece together some of the concepts behind the training. It went something like this:

Most of us don't experience life at all. We generalize or conceptualize—"I don't feel well" or "I'm tired"—instead of being specific about what is happening, for instance "I have tenseness in the left side of my jaw" or "I'm avoiding doing the dishes."

When we break down our beliefs to deal in a more direct way with our experience, the barriers to experience simply disappear.

Among other things, the processes offer us the opportunity to look into our minds to see the beliefs that get us stuck and the automatic behavior, and past conditioning, that prevent us from acting responsibly. Stewart's example was "When you meet someone new, such as a sixty-five-year-old man with gray hair, do you see him as he is or do you immediately notice his resemblance to your father, grandfather, or someone else? The little voice inside you that points up the resemblance is the automatic and unconscious behavior that keeps you from seeing and experiencing him this very moment as he really is."

While Stewart was talking, I remembered a Jules Feiffer cartoon that shows a disembodied head trying to connect with its body. In the last frame, it almost reaches the body but can't quite get securely attached. The message was clear: We've gotten into our heads at the expense of our bodies. Noticing how we feel, what we feel, and where we feel—whether through est processes or any other technique—is the mark of being truly alive.

Stewart put it another way. "If we can have a direct experience without it being limited by our thoughts, our attitudes, by that little voice, and if we can become aware of that little voice, we can then become spontaneous instead of mechanical."

And from Marcia: "You get the space to have a direct experience of who you are, not through your mind, your thoughts, your attitudes, your feelings, or through your understanding. You get the space to stop evaluating and judging and, instead, react to life spontaneously."

After an hour-and-a-half the seminar leaders called for a break. We were told to look for people with blue-edged name tags who would happily tell us about their est experiences. The saved will communicate with the heathen, I mused as I headed for the door and a cigarette.

A lovely young blue-tagged woman (a secretary) approached me. I asked her what est had done for her. "I still have the same problems," she answered me directly, "but I see them differently and I'm having more fun."

A fortyish lawyer told me that after hating his father for thirty years, they had been reunited in his father's old age. There was a hint of a tear in his eye as he said this.

Alongside me a woman asked if est would interfere with her therapy. The graduate explained that est is est and therapy is therapy, and that she could have both.

As I headed back into the room a lively and pretty woman

buttonholed me to share that she would never be the same again. "I have a new awareness of what I do and it's working. My life is . . ." She paused to search for the right word, which turned out to be, again, "working."

When we were settled in our chairs, a well-dressed businessman immediately complained about the hard sell. He compared it to selling toothpaste. To which Stewart replied, "We want to share the training with you. And we want to present it so that you get to make the choice about participating or not. We have no investment or need to make you take the training." Marcia had said earlier, "We in est don't feel we have the only way. And we think that est has shown it is *a* way."

We were then invited to ask questions. Marcia quoted a Werner aphorism: "In life, understanding is the booby prize." There were titters through the audience as hands shot up. They all wanted to understand, regardless.

Is est anti-intellectual? Stewart answered, "We use words to wrap our experiences in. One of the objectives of the training is to allow you to begin to listen to where the words come from instead of just hearing the words." The questioner looked confused but politely sat down. I thought of how so many of us cling, like drowning men, to old ideas without looking at the truth of our lives right now.

A tense young woman wanted to know if, after est, a couple can "come together more" or if their relationship might get worse. Marcia answered in her no-nonsense voice. "Either. *And* whichever way it turns out people seem to get value and nourishment from it as a result of the training." She added that if they come to the training together they won't be permitted to sit together.

Her use of the word "and" jarred me. I had been hearing it all evening in places where I would have consistently used "but." As I ventured further into est I soon found that everyone seemed to use "and"—usually emphasized—in places where I didn't expect it and didn't understand it. Eventually I *got* that it implies that alternatives exist, as opposed to the either/or thinking that rules both our language and our behavior but limit you both by word and attitude.

The money question was raised by an efficient-looking elderly man. "Who owns the common stock?" est is profit-making, came the answer, but not in Hawaii. *And* the intention is not to make a profit; it all goes back into expansion. A man in the back called out that $250 sounded cheap to him. "My wife spent $3,000 this year on therapy," he announced, "and she's still crazy." I saw heads nodding around the room. I guessed that hundreds of thousands of dollars had gone down in therapy from the group assembled that evening. And that many of them saw themselves as still crazy.

The questions rolled on. Yes, deaf and dumb people can take the training. . . . No, age is no barrier; we had a woman take it who is ninety-four and we have trainings for children as young as six. . . . Yes, if you have a medical problem about going to the bathroom you can bring a note from your doctor and you can go to the bathroom when you need to. . . . No, you don't have to do anything during the training except be there. . . . Yes, it's true that we ask you to refrain from alcohol, marijuana, medications—except those prescribed by your physician—sleeping pills, etc., immediately before and during the training. . . .

It struck me that a disproportionate number of questions concerned toileting and eating. After I had been through the training, I was less surprised by these questions. The trainer had repeatedly reminded us that we all live our lives as though we are tubes—our primary concern being what goes in and comes out of our bodies, "Food and shit, shit and food," the litany went. It was all uncomfortably familiar.

"Is it brainwashing?" someone who had just read an anti-est article asked. The answer: "In my experience it is not. Each person sees from their own point of view. The author of that article had a particular point of view and what I can tell you is that what the article had to say is not my experience of the training." The article, in fact, had been scathing, and est, true to form, never put it down.

People began to come to est's defense. A middle-aged man said he was there because a friend who took the training was now doing hang gliding. Before, he was scared of everything.

Another said, "I've gone all around the world to get enlightened. And this is where I've wound up."

A woman shared that a friend of hers had never *seen* flowers before. And another complained that taking the training was like buying real estate in Florida without seeing it.

Each person who spoke got a positive response: thank you, fabulous, wonderful, O.K. Astute and clever remarks received no more points than dumb ones. Everyone was acknowledged equally. No one got an argument or a defense or a deliberate evasion from the seminar leaders. If they didn't know the answer, they simply said so.

The large guest seminars wind down with more anecdotes and finally a sales pitch. There are usually a handful of spaces left in the next couple of trainings and then nothing until three or four months thence. People are told they need to reserve their space in advance by making a deposit of $30; and that trainings fill very quickly. There's a sense that if you don't act right away you might miss the greatest opportunity of your life. (There are about 12,000 people across the country pre-enrolled in the training. In most cities, the wait for a training is two to three months. Sometimes additional trainings are added, giving people the opportunity to register for a training only a few weeks away.) When the seminars are over, there are invariably lines around the sign-up tables. I understand that 15 to 20 percent of those attending usually enroll: Happiness is contagious.

The regular guest seminars, which are given every evening when there is a graduate seminar (in New York this is up to five times a week), and which attract several dozen to several hundred people at a time, offer the bonus of a mini-process, a version of which is duplicated on the following pages. Doing this process is an excellent way to get a sense of at least one aspect of the training.

This mini-process resembles but is not actually a training process. (I cannot ethically reveal the training processes, nor would I choose to do so, because I feel that knowing them in advance significantly reduces the experience of them in the training.)

In sharing this with you, I want also to recommend that you experience it with a friend. Have the other person read the instructions to you rather than read to yourself. Merely reading the words is meaningless and in no way can convey the potential for the experience. Each of the instructions should be followed by a pause to allow the participant time to look and be able to respond to himself. If you're not interested in going into this experience at this particular time, I suggest that you just skip to the next chapter, perhaps to return to this place at another, more leisurely, time.

The process begins:

Please uncross your arms, uncross your legs, take everything off your lap, get into a comfortable position, relax and close your eyes. Thank you.

The first thing I would like you to do is to bring the chair that you are sitting on within your space and experience what it's like for you sitting there in that chair. Good.

Now expand your space to include the person or persons sitting on either side of you. Thank you.

Notice if you have any attitudes or opinions or emotions or thoughts about the person or persons sitting next to you, and, if you do, notice what they are. Good.

Now keep expanding your space or your experience of you to include all the people here in the room, and notice what it's like for you sitting here with these people. Thank you.

Notice if you have any attitudes about the group, or if you think the group has a particular attitude, and if you do, notice what that is. Fine.

Now keep expanding your space to include the whole room. Recall the floor, the walls, forms, textures, and colors. Notice the sounds and smells, notice what it's like for you, what your experience is of being here in this room. Good.

Now recall a time when you were really happy with someone and notice what that experience was like for you. Thank
you.

Now recall a time when you really communicated with
someone and they really got that communication and notice
what that experience was like for you. Great.

Now recall another time when someone else was really
happy with you. Get a very clear picture of an incident when
someone else was really happy with you, and notice how you
carried your body.

Notice how you walked, how you talked, how you smiled,
how you tilted your head. Notice how you experienced you
when someone else was really happy with you. Thank you.

Now recall another time when you were really happy with
someone. Get a clear picture of that, allow yourself to experience what it was like for you when you were really happy
with someone else. Just keep experiencing that; notice what
you were saying, how you were feeling, what the other person
is saying, what they're doing. Good. Now bring a stranger
into the experience and notice what happens to the experience. What happens when a stranger comes in. How are you
holding your body now? How do you feel now? What are
your thoughts now or your attitude now that a stranger is
present? Thank you.

Just keep your eyes closed, we are going to do a couple
more things. First, just go through your body and notice if
you have any tension. You might check out that area behind
your neck, between your shoulders. You might even like to
wiggle your head around a little. Great.

Notice the area between your eyes, at the top of your nose.
Just notice if that's tense or not. You may want to take your
hand and rub your forehead a little. Great.

Now just notice your arms and your legs and see if they
are in any position. You might want to shake your arms out,
notice if they are crossed. If they are, uncross them. Very
good.

Now take a look and notice if your jaw is clamped tight and, if it is, see if it is O.K. with you to release it. Just let it relax. Thank you.

O.K. Now what I'd like you to do is take your hands and rub them back and forth on the chair you're sitting on and notice what comes up for you to experience while you are rubbing your hands back and forth on the chair. Notice if you feel silly or irritated or confused or if you are doing it just a little bit so that the person next to you doesn't know that you are doing it; notice if you are afraid of touching hands with the person next to you. Notice if you are wondering about what the significance of rubbing your hands on the chair is. Keep rubbing your hands till I say stop. O.K. Stop rubbing your hands.

Now take your feet and rub them back and forth on the carpet. See if you can tell what the color of the carpet is through the bottoms of your feet. What color does the carpet feel like? Good.

The last thing I would like you to do is to get a sense of the space you would like to be in with yourself. Just get a clear sense of how you would like to experience you, and when you've got a sense of the space you would like to be in, and you feel really good about that space, so good that you can't help but smile, then what I want you to do is to smile and open your eyes into that space. Good.

In the small guest seminar I attended, the seminar leader suggested that we might want to share what we experienced in the process. One man admitted that he had trouble finding a happy experience. Another shared that he had *thought* he was happy when his kids were born but he realized that that wasn't what he had just experienced. A third shared that he got that he wouldn't let himself have happiness. And a fourth confessed that absolutely nothing happened to her.

A woman told us that she couldn't let the stranger into her space because she was in a compromising position. She got that she felt guilty about her sexual pleasure.

For another the stranger turned out to be the most influential person in his life. And so it went.

For me, the most fascinating aspect of this exercise was the multiplicity of individual experiences. No two people saw or felt the same things. Most were amazed at the variety and wealth of the material they were able to call forth.

The leader (in this case, Monique) pointed out that each of us is different because each of us makes different choices. It is the inability to choose, she explained, that keeps us stuck in our lives. When you make a choice, your life moves forward. The choice usually boils down to a simple "yes" or "no." "I don't know" is also a choice—the choice to evade responsibility.

A woman wanted to know what kind of choice she makes when she is depressed. A lot of people turned to her; it's a universal problem. The leader answered: "If you're depressed, you can choose to have your depression; you can take responsibility for it. Or you can choose to resist it and be at its effect, helpless."

Monique, who is an airline stewardess, concluded this particular seminar with a confession. "I haven't the foggiest notion what est is all about. I only know my life works better."

I, too, hadn't the foggiest notion of what it was all about. But I knew that I wanted it. The way I once knew that I wanted an orgasm before I had ever had sex: Everyone had told me how terrific it was, but no one could tell me how it worked or what it really felt like.

I found out that orgasms were worth experiencing. I would trust that est was, too.

Father Joseph Brendler

Father Joseph Brendler, thirty-two, is a hospital chaplain, pastoral counselor, and on the faculty of New Orleans' Notre Dame Seminary. He is a large and impressive man whose honesty I found disarming.

I was tremendously nervous before I flew to San Francisco to take the training. I had no idea what to expect.

The most important thing I got from est is acceptance of myself where I am negative. What has happened is that I have lost my fantasies about myself and the world. Now I see things as they are. Before I had this need to always make progress, to be perfect. That's the whole bag people get into the clergy for.

Now I simply accept the things I cannot change—and even the things I don't want to. (My office, for example, is usually a mess. I'm supposed to keep it neat, but now I just let it be.) The "supposed to" is gone from my life.

At est I got that I am satisfied with being the way I am. I don't have to be the warm, supportive, bubbly person that I believed my role as a priest calls for. I can be grumpy. It's O.K. to be grumpy. I can be the way I feel and I can be honest about it. I can also give other people the responsibility to be the way they feel.

As a pastoral counselor I am less demanding now of my counselees. I used to want them to move along, to change. The key word really is responsibility—me for my life, they for theirs. I know now that I can assist, but I don't help.*

I accept the people who come to see me the way they are. At the same time I am more confronting than I used to be.

* See Glossary for distinction.

I am no longer afraid to tell it like it is. It is O.K. to be honest, to be the way you are.

est gave me the *experience* of what theology has been *telling* me.

Blessing is acceptance and affirmation of the fact that others are all right the way they really are. I never really got that before. I could see that people looked blessed, but I didn't have the power to bless because of my desire to change people.

The great mystics who were wrapped up with God had that complete acceptance. I just knew about it through faith. But now I am developing more spirituality because of my new ability to let go and stop controlling others. And to experience reality the way it is.

The last night of the training it all made sense to me. Until then it was total confusion. I finally could feel—not think or rationalize—that the responsibility to accept or not accept others and myself was mine. I knew without a doubt that I couldn't change.

Giving up that illusion of control threw me into a deep depression for a month after I returned to New Orleans following the training. Previously, I had been in therapy in New Orleans with a psychiatrist. He helped me through that month of depression and now I have given up therapy.

Soon after the training I was scheduled to give a weekend retreat for about forty men in northern Louisiana. As I was preparing my sermon the connection dawned; I saw that letting go of life, relinquishing my control, was the answer. That entire weekend retreat I wrote about my est experience without identifying est. That was the turning point. Putting that weekend together pulled the whole est experience together for me and gave me new enthusiasm and new energy in my life.

I haven't any idea how the training works, how what happened to me happened and what motivates me to feel the way I do now. I only know that I feel different than I ever have before. Sure, I still go up and down. I have moods like anybody else. But it's O.K. I simply experience my moods as they happen. And my relationships in every area of my life have improved because I can experience them. I no longer try to control them.

I handle confession differently, too. The theology of grace, that you don't have to earn salvation, I had previously accepted. But I still measured people by my standards. I was condescending.

I'm really in touch with compassion now. Beneath the garbage of fear that we all have, we really want to be good, warm, friendly, and loving. Even though a person might be a thief, cruel, mean, I can sense the lonely person underneath.

My idea of right and wrong is simply that if one does injury to another person, that is wrong. Judging something as sinful is judging that someone has hurt another person.

I am much closer to God now. I see God's relationship to us. It really doesn't matter what we do; God's love of us doesn't change. In the parable of the Prodigal Son, which I had never really understood, I identified with the long-suffering elder son and was angry at the acceptance of the younger son. Now I see that it is O.K. for me to be this way and it doesn't matter.

I wouldn't trade my est experience for the world. Looking back I see that I was so uptight that if I hadn't paid the $250 in advance I would have left after that first weekend and never returned.

3

Beliefs

"Belief is a disease."

—*Werner Erhard*

Werner says, "The truth believed is a lie. If you go around preaching the truth, you are lying. The truth can only be experienced. This illuminates the old Zen koan: 'Those who know don't tell and those who tell don't know.' The horrible part about it is that the truth is so damn believable, people usually believe it instead of experiencing it."

Because so much of what est is about is related to people's beliefs, to what they think "the truth" is, I digress here to explore what est calls "belief systems."

Everyone has belief systems, formed when we were children. Some samples: Daddies go to work and Mommies stay home and take care of the children. If you're good, you go to heaven. People have to eat three square meals a day to stay healthy. Being in love is not having to say you're sorry. I must be strong or nobody will love me. Hard work is good (bad) for you. *Ad infinitum.*

Our beliefs about romantic love, and what a man-woman relationship should be, as opposed to the reality of what it actually is, are probably the main reason why the divorce rate in this country continues to soar. The belief about the relationship seldom meshes with what goes on between any couple on a daily basis. est defines love as "giving someone the space to be the way they are and the way they are not."

Some of the beliefs I grew up with are: blond, blue-eyed children are prettier than those who, like me, have curly brown hair and green eyes. The way to be happy is to acquire a lot of college degrees and a lot of money. Men are weak. It's just as easy to marry a rich man as a poor man. Tears and headaches are a woman's lot in life—sometimes curable by long hot baths.

est allows us to see that not until we separate what we *believe* from what we *experience* can we begin to run our own lives.

The belief systems est talks about (called parental injunctions in Transactional Analysis) are the concepts we use to run our lives. The problem with a belief is that we take it to be truth—and get stuck in it. That means that most of us persist in thinking and doing what we learned long ago, rather than acting out of our experience in response to whatever is happening now.

A classic story illustrates this point: A young bride regularly cuts off the ends of the ham before putting it in the pan to bake. After watching her do this several times, her husband asks her why. She answers that her mother always did it that way. So the husband asks the mother-in-law why she cut off the ends of the ham. To which she replies, "Because my mother always did it that way." The old grandmother is still alive, so he visits her one day and asks the same question. "I cut the ends off the ham," she explains, "because we were very poor and had only one pan for all our baking. To get a large ham into the small pan, we had to cut the ends off."

Most of us are cutting the ends off something in our lives to fit it into a pan that's no longer too small for it. est tells us we are robots, machines, stuck in the soap opera of our lives, obsessed with the same four or five problems we've always had, only dressed in new clothes.

For example, you skin your knee at five and mother says, "Don't cry; crying is bad," so you don't cry. When you are sixteen, you break your leg skiing, and you keep a stiff upper lip because you are a good boy or girl, which means you don't cry. Then, at twenty-one, a relationship with someone ends and you still don't cry. After a while the more you repress whatever it is you are feeling, the more your consciousness shuts down, just like a trap door. You are barely alive. You function mechanically. In some cases, you're successful at it. But mechanical success is not any more satisfying than failure.

Psychotherapy has always been concerned with the way people are run by what *was* rather than what *is,* and how to free people from the prison of their past. The difference between est and therapy is that therapy is concerned with curing people of illness and est is concerned with offering people—sick and healthy—an experience of themselves. est makes no claims at all.

In an interview with Marcia Seligson,* Werner said, "A belief system is myth, created by knowledge or data without experience. If you experience something, it is real for you, and if you communicate it to somebody, it's real for them. If they now tell it to somebody else, it's a lie—belief without the component of experience.

"Now belief is very powerful; you can cure with it or kill with it. I earned my living for years training people to believe in themselves. The problem is that beliefs are a state of hypnosis, automatic, and totally non-nurturing. Like, the degree to which I have beliefs about women, I can't see you; not only that, but I can *prove* to you, from my beliefs, that what I think I see is actually true." Werner later said, "That there are people out there believing in us, in me, is a failure of est that we are working to correct."

He distinguishes between looking for answers outside of ourselves and what's going on within us. "If I get the idea that God is going to save me, therefore I'm all right, that's salvation. If I get the idea that nothing's going to save me, therefore I'm all right, that's enlightenment. . . . People get involved in therapy, groups, and movements to get better. That's not what people get from us."

Before and after the pre-training, and again during the first days of the training, I asked people what they *expected* to get out of est. A lot of them told me they wanted to fall in love or get married or get divorced. Some spoke about improving job

* *New Times* (October 18, 1974).

situations, family relationships, or the state of their health. Others were more general: "to make better decisions"; "to have more self-confidence"; "to be more together and less confused." One attractive young man told me he wanted either to find a way to grow hair on his chest or learn to accept that he was attractive and virile without it; he was serious.

What they all had in common was a set of expectations. They believed their happiness was dependent on more love, more money, more sex, more self-confidence, or more chest hair. Each one had a belief system which related satisfaction to something he or she was striving for. None of them saw their happiness as a function of accepting what *is,* apart and separate from what *was* and what is to come.

I remember an occasion, shortly after I was divorced, when I spent a weekend alone—and in one of the worst depressions of my entire life. I was depressed because I believed that an attractive, vital woman should be spending that holiday weekend "having fun," which included every notion I had ever had of what fun was all about. I felt myself a failure because I was alone, because I hadn't been invited anywhere, and because, above all, I didn't have a man in my life at the time. That same holiday weekend eight years later found me holed up in a hotel room writing this book—alone and happy in the moment of doing.

"Belief is a structure which can contain very little information in terms of making it useful in one's consciousness or well-being," says Werner.

The alternative to belief is what the yogis call witness and what est calls observation. "Observation," Werner says, "has nothing to do with my senses, perceptions, or my belief system. It has to do with my direct experience. . . . Don Juan gives it another name: stopping the world."

When we're convinced that someone is wrong we're often quarreling with his observations because they don't mesh with our beliefs. Everyone has his own experience of anything and everything, and, in addition, his own way of conceptualizing.

I feel that it's because formal religion has become so removed from our own personal experience that our churches are empty today. "God believed," I've heard Werner say, "is a lie." A beautiful young woman from New Orleans who works as a hospital chaplain told me her faith was deeply reinforced after the training.

"I had given up the church in which I had been raised," she shared, "because there was a lot of talk about God there that didn't mean anything to me. I was studying primitive religions; they were much more involved with feelings. Now, since est, I've had the most incredible sense of mission—and of God. I am back in divinity school. And I am going to church again. est brought me back to my religious feelings in a new and deeper way."

Werner says that "life could be considered to be three feet long, and the first two feet, eleven and three-quarter inches are about the material aspects of life (e.g., food, clothing, and shelter) and what we call the psychological needs. You need someone to love you and probably somebody to love. You need self-esteem, recognition, the respect of others.

"After people become sophisticated enough in their development to fill their needs, to begin to look at what it means to fill one's needs, and even to begin to realize that there's no true satisfaction in merely filling one's needs, then they begin to look for what's beyond that. And that is the last quarter inch—that's what consciousness is about for me—the last quarter inch."

It is this last quarter inch that this book is all about. And to *get* it, you're going to have to suspend some of your beliefs. "est talk" may sound like double-talk to non-est graduates.

If some of what's in the pages ahead seems like non sequiturs, or, worse, crazy, I suggest that you check out your belief systems. If you can separate yourself from what you're *used* to thinking, then you will see the est language as simply an experiential way of putting words together and the est training as a way to lead you to an experience of yourself.

Jim

Jim, thirty-four, is an attractive and successful advertising executive who commutes between New York and Los Angeles. He was raised in Idaho, where both of his parents were schoolteachers.

I had thought I'd come a long way from Idaho. Until I took est.

I took the training after a close friend who was miserable most of his life went through it. Never had I seen such a drastic change in anyone in such a short time.

The point was that his problems were the same but the way he dealt with them was totally different. I hesitated about going, though, because it seemed too pat, too easy, a panacea, the kind of thing that I had always guarded myself against—that some one person had all the answers. Fortunately I made up my mind to do it before I went to the guest seminar. The hard sell, the push, the broad grin, too much conviviality—everything I detest about organized things—were all there.

When I went into est, I saw that even though my life was generally on an even keel, in close personal relationships I was messed up. When I got too close, it didn't work. The easiest relationship for me was playing big brother—give and give and give, hoping I might get. I used to say I was a perfect Pisces; I was hypersensitive to other people's feelings and I became whoever they wanted me to be. I was a mask. I'm so good at this sort of thing that I once sat through a friend's suicide attempt to prove to myself what a good guy I was.

During the training, I hated sitting still. But when we got to the Danger Process I began to open up. The tears kept rolling down while the trainer stood in front of me telling me to let it out, to experience it. He told the group, "Look at this big man and see how he is willing to expose himself." To me, what he was saying was that the football-hero façade that I had always carried with me was just junk.

Frankly I was relieved when the training was over. There was a lot of physical and emotional stress.

After the training, when friends would call for my usual dose of sympathy, I found that I could no longer be that remote, level-headed, astute advice-giver I had always been.

The week after the training, on a business trip, I found I could allow an angry client his space to be, which gave me a new freedom to define mine. I simply don't fall back on my old rote responses. I get less uptight around people who I feel want something from me. And, since I've stopped giving clients anything and everything they want, I get less pressure from them.

One night this week I had another realization from the seed planted in the training. I was late for a date—my life is pretty pressured—and rushing to pick her up I suddenly became aware of the tension pulsing through my body, the shallowness of my breathing, how my fists were clenched, how my body was hunched over the wheel of the car. I wouldn't have noticed it before and I certainly wouldn't have connected it with my feelings.

As soon as I started looking at it—my posture, muscles, eyes—it changed. By the time I got to my date's house, it was all gone. At another time I would have walked in and most likely picked a fight, or hated the evening.

My parents are special to me now, and I'm going to tell them that. I've come to realize that love expands your space. Now I can share with them; I can tell them about my fears and what's gone wrong in my life. They've known nothing important about me since I left home at eighteen.

A friend last night shared with me that he has a new record, new dope, new brandy; that's his way. I didn't respond in my old "Gee, that's wonderful" way. By the end of the evening we were really communicating—not about "things."

I don't proselytize about est. I don't especially like the clannishness of the volunteers, the recruiting, the mass hysteria of the guest seminars. I know there are a lot of people for whom est is a complete way of life. I don't support that. I don't recommend that people go. And it's changed my life.

4

The Training

"Follow the instructions and take what you get."

—est koan

"Life's . . . a tale told by an idiot, full of sound and fury, signifying nothing."

—William Shakespeare

All eyes were focused on the handsome young man standing at the back of the room. His face contorted, his eyes red, he pleaded to be allowed to go to the bathroom. The trainer simply stared at him until, after a while, the young man shut up and sat down. No one had physically barred his way. Nor had anyone told him that he couldn't leave. It was his choice to remain in the room.

About ten minutes later he raised his hand for a microphone. "I want you to know," he announced, "that I just peed in my pants." In a crisp, staccato voice, he added: "And it really doesn't matter." Two hundred and forty-nine people cheered and applauded.

It was at that moment that I knew I would make it through the training. And *get* it.

What follows is my experience of the est training based on my own personal experience and the experience of those who have shared with me.*

* Everyone who now takes the est training is asked to sign an agreement not to divulge the material of the training, including, but not limited to, the names of the participants and their remarks. An est trainer clarified

BEFORE

The training unofficially begins with the "pre-training," on Monday evening preceding the first weekend, which is recommended but not required. The pre-training, in effect, revs you up for the training. It presents the ground rules for the training, gets you used to some of what's to come, and leaves you eager for more. I loved it. I left it smiling—and with homework. Neither of which, incidentally, prepared me for what I was to experience in the training itself.

The night of the pre-training I was back in a hotel ballroom again, this one at the New York Statler Hilton. (In all of my est experience so far I must have been in more than two dozen hotel ballrooms, draped and carpeted in the usual shades of gold, crimson, or blue and lit by massive chandeliers. The new location for enlightenment, I mused.) Smiling faces led me from the lobby to the elevator to the ballroom, whereupon more smiling faces checked me in, tagged me, and directed me to sit "in the front-most, center-most chair."

While I smoked my last cigarette for the evening I looked over the group I would be holed up with for the next two weekends. They might have been an intermission crowd at a Lincoln Center ballet performance. Most were well-dressed in business clothes, and a few were carefully casual in fashionable jean

the nature of my commitment. I could share my *experience* of est, which is exactly what I had set out to do. I regard this book as an agreement kept, *and* its point of view is strictly my own. I would like to add here that my description of the training is a compilation of several experiences. I want to say also that a few of my est friends feel that knowing about the training in advance has a negative effect on the experience. I share that. And I disagree with it. A friend of mine who took it after a friend of his had given him a day-by-day rundown of what happens told me that on the first day of his own training he kept damning the informant for "spoiling the training for me. I knew what was coming next, and I felt gypped." By the end of the second day he *got* that he was spoiling his own experience. The training turned out to be an incredible breakthrough for him. I believe that knowing about the training can change your experience of it only if you choose to have your experience changed by it.

outfits. All appeared to be serious, thoughtful, and intelligent. They ranged in age from late teens to (I later learned) mid-seventies. Some appeared nervous, some not, the rest so well masked that it was impossible to tell.

Right off, after we were all seated, the pre-training seminar leader (the trainer is there only for the weekends and the post-training) announced that whatever he would tell us was told to us because "it works." "Werner only uses what works," he explained. And, later, "Whatever is in the training is there because Werner found out that's what works."

This was to be the first of many times that I would hear someone quote Werner as though he were God. "Werner says . . ." is the final word at est, from the trainers down to the pre-trainers.

"Now," the leader continued, "I'll tell you who you will meet at est." I immediately had visions of a string of celebrities come to add their testimonials to the dozens I had already heard.

The people we were going to meet, he said, were ourselves. First, we were told, we would see our social selves, the person each of us thinks he is. This is the self that's familiar and comfortable. And automatic. Its favorite line goes something like, "Don't call me on my act and I won't call you on yours." Next we would meet the person we're afraid to find out we are . . . that "terrible" person we try to hide with our social selves—what is hidden under the mask we label "personality." And finally—he grinned—we would meet who we really are. He looked us over, knowingly. In so doing, he acknowledged that we hadn't the vaguest idea of what he was talking about. But that we eventually would.

We then went on to the agreements, which are a critical part of the est experience. The agreements are not what we can and can't do throughout the training. Rather, they're what we *agree* we can and can't do throughout the training. There is no policing of the rules, nor is there punishment in the traditional sense of the word for breaking them. "Life works to the degree to which you keep your agreements," the leader told us.

The ground rules are read seriously from a loose-leaf binder.

Always. Lest there be any question that this is serious business, we are told right away in a loud and stern voice that there would be no talking. All fidgeting stopped. All eyes were front center on the man we later dubbed among ourselves "the mortician." We listened to the words for the first time. It was like listening to a death sentence. What price enlightenment? I wondered as I took it all in.

For a start, we, as trainees, are to agree not to take alcohol, marijuana, sleeping pills, uppers, downers, or anything else that is not medication a doctor says we have to take. That includes tranquilizers and all the other prescription mood drugs. We *may* take coffee, tea, cigarettes. And birth-control pills. The last gets a laugh from everyone except the poker-faced leader.

We also agree not to have a timepiece in the training room; to go to the bathroom only at bathroom breaks; not to eat at any time other than the single meal break; to be there on time and to stay until the trainer decides we've gotten what we need to get for that day. On and on. I notice that my shoulders are hunched, my hands clenched. We go on making agreements.

We will stayed seated unless called on. We will not sit with anyone we knew before the training. We will not talk unless we're sharing, in which case we will talk into a microphone (which we're taught in detail how to use). We agree to wear our name tags at all times when we're in the room and always keep them visible (people with long hair are to pin them in the center of their chests). We agree not to move our chairs from their positions unless instructed to do so. . . .

Finally the leader said that if we wanted to *get* the training, all we needed to do was keep our soles in the room and follow instructions. He pointed to the bottom of his shoe in case any of us thought he meant something more esoteric.

I looked around at the people who were taking this in. The man on my left was a Park Avenue surgeon whose nephew, children, and wife had taken the training. Behind me was a well-known art director of a leading magazine. Another man, with whom I had a friend in common, was the producer of a national television news program. There was also a well-known actor, a woman president of an advertising agency, and a physicist—to name just a few of the outwardly successful among us. We all sat there, ostensibly passive, until the entire list had been read. Then the hands shot up.

Most of the questions, not surprisingly, were about what went in and came out of the body. This corroborated the tube theory expounded in the guest seminars, which would be repeated during the training. Toileting got the most attention. "Not being able to go to the bathroom is unreasonable," one man complained. "Yes," came the matter-of-fact answer. "It's unreasonable. That's what the training is. Unreasonable. The opposite not of reason but of reasonableness."

Other questions dealt with food and physical comfort. A woman asked for, and was given, permission to bring a pillow to the training. On Saturday a number of people showed up clutching pillows in their arms. "Legitimatized security blankets," I thought.

Werner later told me that although the physical discomfort was a valuable aspect of the training, it was not essential and, since people got stuck on it, for many months now there have been shorter hours and more frequent breaks without any difference in results.

After the rules came the pitfalls, which were all the traps we would get ourselves into; while nothing can keep you from *getting it,* the pitfalls would be barriers to the growth process. At one time or another, I was to fall into each of them. At the moment, though, I was convinced I was beyond them. In fact, the more rigorous and unyielding the whole process sounded, the more I felt I could endure it. Those were the kinds of barriers I loved to hurdle. The barriers I was unprepared for, which would almost be my undoing, were the soft, pliable things: boredom, sleepiness, feelings that nothing was happening.

The evening moved through more data and a couple of exercises. One involved introducing ourselves. We were told that when most of us encounter somebody on the street we're more aware of what their shoes look like than their eyes. Everyone found that one funny. I was noticing that we laughed longest and loudest when we were most uncomfortable. Being made aware of our acts—our fronts to the world—produced the most discomfort of all.

By the time the pre-training evening session was over, I felt good about what was to come. I had laughed a lot. And nothing seemed beyond my considerable repertoire of responses to encounter/feeling/self-examination-type growth experiences. It was a lovely, if short-lived, delusion.

I noticed later on my way back to Philadelphia that my jaws ached and my shoulders and neck felt as if they had weights hanging from them. If I had thought earlier that it was going to be painless or that I could somehow remain detached, I now was forced to reconsider what I was getting myself into.

THE FIRST WEEKEND

Saturday dawned gray and merciless. I debated how much to eat and drink for breakfast, given that neither our bathroom nor our meal break might come until evening. I settled on two cups of coffee and made a note to stop in the ladies' room just before the training began. Then I dressed, in layers; I had heard that the training rooms are kept cold to keep people awake. (I found out later that this was not true; the training rooms are kept at a constant temperature of 70–73 degrees. The apparent changes in temperature are merely changes in people's experience.)

The hotel this time was the New York Sheraton. All I saw of it that morning were the gold-colored name tags graced with the est orchid leaves worn by volunteer greeters. Outside the training room I made my way past more name tags to find my own and get my bearings.

The previous Wednesday we had all been exhorted to make eye contact with people. You would hardly have known it by the performance that morning. Except for a dozen or so couples, everyone else had staked out an isolated hunk of carpeting as his or her turf, from which beneath lowered eyelids the quiet confusion was surveyed. Here and there people chatted distractedly. In a corner a young woman twisted a cord on her handbag and seemed about to cry. A toothless man in his middle years, who I later learned was an elevator operator, kept loosening and tightening his tie. The successful were indistinguishable from the less successful, with most people dressed in the weekend uniform of our time: blue jeans.

The doors to the training room opened at 7:30. We were reminded, again, to sit in "the front-most, center-most chair." Those of us who had disregarded instructions to leave our watches home now checked them at the door. The mood was somber. To break the heavy silence, I started a conversation with a good-looking man alongside me.

He had come to est, he told me, on the recommendation of a woman friend. The friend had been, like him, an advertising account executive. During the training, she *got* that she was frigid. She subsequently left her high-status and well-paying job to work full time producing pornography films. I thought he was putting me on. He wasn't.

Promptly at 8:30 the doors were closed. What the trainer later called "the roller coaster ride" had begun.

After a re-reading of the ground rules by a training supervisor in the by-now-familiar humorless, no-nonsense style, the trainer—the star—arrived and strode purposefully to the platform at the front of the room.

He wasted no time in getting down to business. There were no introductions, no preliminaries, no niceties. He glowered at us and announced that we were all assholes. I knew it was coming but I flinched anyway. A woman in front of me began to shake.

"You are an asshole," he repeated loudly. "You are a machine. Your life doesn't work. You're an asshole because you pretend that it does." He paced from one end of the platform to the other, punctuating each staccato statement with a thrust of his arm.

The verbal flagellation continued. "You people are here today because all of your strategies, your smart-ass theories, and all the rest of your shit hasn't worked for you. In this training you're going to find out you've been acting like assholes. All of your fucking cleverness and self-deception have gotten you nowhere."

As I noticed people squirm I was delighted that I wasn't bothered by the four-letter words; I had done enough encounter to handle the fuck-shit-cunt routine like a street kid. Later I learned that people occasionally leave the training ostensibly because the language is too raw for them. The trainer's response to a woman who questioned the use of these words was " 'Spaghetti' and 'fuck' are the same. They're only words. The difference is the significance you add to them."

It seemed to me that the idea was to reduce us to pulp, to attack us where we're most vulnerable, to eventually have us identify those areas of our lives that don't produce results. "When you reach a critical mass of observation," Werner says, "things can begin to disappear."

I looked around and noted that all but one of the exit doors had signs across them saying "NO EXIT"; the other door had an est volunteer in front of it to prevent entry from outside. Although the doors are not locked and no one is ever barred from leaving, I resigned myself to accepting that I was going to feel trapped, like it or not.

I turned my full attention to the trainer, Stewart Emery. Incredibly handsome, his suntanned face was set off by a luxurious head of silver-gray hair. I judged him to be about thirty-seven. At that moment he didn't look like someone I could snuggle up with, but I saw the potential. Many women friends who trained with some of the other trainers developed crushes on them; it seems to be part of the syndrome—the need for transference and identification.

Stewart told us what we needed to do to *get* the training. "If you stay in the room during the training, you'll get it. If you sleep through the training, as long as you are in this room sleeping, you'll get it.

"Trying to understand the training, using your head to understand the training, and trying to figure it all out are inappropriate ways to get this training. What you need to do to get the training is just to follow instructions and take what you get."

I was surprised about the permission to nod out. I also wondered how it was possible in those straight-back chairs lined up with no space right and left and only a foot or so in front. When I heard the first blissful snores that afternoon, and dozed off myself the next morning, I stopped wondering.

Stewart said, "The truth puts people to sleep. It goes right to what's unconscious in them, and most people are unconscious. For the truth to get to the truth in people, it has to get through the unconscious. So if you can make people uncomfortable in their unconsciousness, enough just to make them aware they *are* unconscious, then you have a better chance of letting some truth strike the truth in them."

The process of getting the truth, whether we got it in a conscious or unconscious state, wasn't going to be painless. "You are going to be intimidated, insulted, frightened, nauseated, enraged, and humiliated," Stewart told us. "You are going to feel every feeling there is to feel." He added that we might vomit, cry, get the shakes. We might also get bellyaches, headaches, and every other kind of ache before the training was over. After he described the training he told us that we now had an opportunity to leave if we wanted. We would get our full tuition back by mail.

It sounded grim—but it was also a challenge. I opted to stay. Others weren't so sure. A dozen or so hands went up, waving frantically.

To share, a trainee raises his hand and waits for the trainer to acknowledge him. He then stands up and waits for a member of the volunteer logistics team to rush forth with a microphone. Then he shares whatever is on his mind: a thought, an experience, an objection, anything that he wants to say, however irrelevant or irreverent. The trainees are instructed to applaud following each sharing. The applause does not signify agreement; it only denotes an acknowledgment that the trainees *got* what the speaker shared.

"I don't like paying $250 to be called an asshole," one man

complained. Stewart flashed an enigmatic, generous smile, his first of the day. "Thank you. I got that." The questioner, looking slightly dazed, sat down.

A woman asked why she couldn't sit next to her husband.

"We do what works for the training," came the blunt response.

A man suddenly got up and headed for the door as if going to the men's room. Stewart asked him if he had forgotten his agreement. He shook his head and returned, flushed and angry, to his seat. A few minutes later he waved his hand for the microphone. "I want to share that any time I want to get out of listening, I go to the bathroom," he told us. Stewart beamed. "You got it about the bathroom."

Hour after hour people shared their points of view. For me it became boring, inane, exhausting. My chair became a jail cell. Of all the genius that had gone into est, I decided, the most ingenious was making people sit and do nothing and become aware of how hard it is to sit and do nothing. I was so accustomed to my physical comfort that to sit for sixty hours in that uncompromising chair seemed, that first couple of hours, something I could not or would not endure. It occurred to me that one of the problems with psychoanalysis was that the required couch was too damn comfortable. As I ruminated on all the objectionable aspects of the seating arrangements I realized that I was on the brink of rage over, of all things, my chair. From that I *got* that I had never let anyone tell me where and when to sit. Or to do anything else, for that matter. I saw that it was going to be almost impossible to avoid myself as long as I remained in the training.

I looked up from my reveries to see est volunteers collecting candy bars. Candy bars, for God's sake! It seemed that people had begun to feel guilt about holding on to goodies they had hidden in their handbags and pockets contrary to their agreement. As one confessed and turned over her cache, others followed. The room was soon a sea of raisins, peanuts, apples, chocolate bars, sandwiches, chewing gum, and an assortment of other forbidden fruits being passed to the waiting volunteers.

The trainer didn't seem to find it funny, but the rest of us were hysterical. Long after the first rush to cleanse ourselves was over, periodically someone would call for a microphone to share that he or she wanted to turn in a guilt-laden edible.

Stewart told us that by the following weekend two-thirds of us would have broken at least one of our agreements. I thought the figure unfairly high and was certain I would not be among the defaulters. I was wrong on both counts. About half the room would stand up the next weekend to acknowledge they had cheated and another large contingent would join them when Stewart said that if we weren't sure if we'd cheated or not, we had. I was in the second group. For a glass of red wine I drank after agreeing not to.

The hours rolled by. Without a watch and with the hotel drapes pinned closed, I had no sense of time. The training was just barely endurable and mostly agonizing. I yearned for activity, interaction, anything to escape from the endless passivity I had been thrust into from a life that was a model of motion.

Stewart continued to hammer away at us. Most of us don't enjoy any degree of aliveness, he pronounced, because we are content to stay at a level of existence where we neither experience nor participate in life. In fact, a lot of us "go unconscious" a lot of the time.

"I tune out while I'm driving," a young woman shared. "Last week I went off the road and narrowly missed a major accident. I woke up and jammed on the brakes in front of a giant elm tree."

"When you are responsible," Stewart thundered, "you find out you just didn't happen to be lying there on the tracks when the train passed through. You are the asshole who put yourself there."

The theme of responsibility pervaded every aspect of the training. In fact, if I were to sum up in a few words what I got from the training data it would be that we are each the cause of our own experience and responsible for everything that happens in our experience.

"I know that your agreement with everyone you know is that

life is tough," he went on, "and that you have to be cool to survive. I want you to get that that doesn't work.

"It also doesn't work to wave the traffic on the freeway in the opposite direction to the way it's going. The traffic doesn't give a damn about you and neither does life. You have to be responsible for the way it is rather than stuck in the way you want it. You set it up this way. Now dig it.

"However it is for you, that's the way you've set it up and no amount of resistance will change that. Now you have a choice. You can keep resisting. Or you can choose it. You can bitch about it. Or you can take responsibility for it. If you are willing to acknowledge that you are cause in the matter, then you can be responsible for it instead of having it run you."

It was powerful stuff and I had a hard time staying with it. I had spent half a lifetime blaming the dissatisfaction of my life on a sad, angry father who had worked his way through Harvard and then went nowhere; on a sad, angry mother who learned to read Greek and Latin at Smith and then spent the rest of her life in a flowered housedress, eating to drown her misery; on an ex-husband who was compulsive, guilt-ridden, and who *tried* but couldn't give me what I wanted; and on bosses and shrinks who never quite lived up to my expectations.

I had begun to see my own responsibility in all this some years before I took the training, but the est experience deepened my experience of being the cause of my life. It also became clearer how I manufactured both my problems and my pleasures.

The irony was that I had never had a problem taking credit for the joys and successes of my life: an early career as a magazine writer, followed by a wonderful stint writing and broadcasting a radio program, followed by a successful public relations career, followed by a return to college in my middle years to study psychology and, subsequently, by my becoming a psychotherapist. Through the past several years, my children have brought me incredible joy in their sanity and ability to function well. My daughter is now at Harvard Business School and my son at the University of Colorado Law School.

It was too painful for me to accept that I, not anyone else, had caused the anguish and despair that had marked so much of my life. While the trainer kept hammering at this theme, and I complained to myself and anyone who would listen to me (outside the training room) about the interminable repetitiveness, eventually my resistance gave way and I *got* it. I got that I had total responsibility for my life—all of it, the happiness and the sorrow. It was—and continues to be—an incredible revelation.

The dinner break late in the evening was a mad dash for a toilet and then some lukewarm soup and chow mein at a nearby Chinese restaurant. I was dizzy, as were the three trainees who had spontaneously become my dinner companions. Strangely enough, I was also not hungry. After visualizing delicacies of every variety throughout the day, I could eat barely half of what was on my plate. I noticed when we were ready to leave that a lot of the plates were still half-full. Either becoming enlightened was stilling our appetites or discovering we were assholes had made us too nauseous to eat.

We swapped stories about what had brought us to est. The one I liked best came from an intense young man who earlier had openly acknowledged that he was homosexual. "It started when I ran into an old friend on the street one day," he told us. "He looked marvelous, sort of blissful. So I said to him, 'What are you on these days?' He'd been into every drug imaginable. And he answered, 'I'm on est these days.' I hadn't heard of that one so, naturally, I asked him if he had any for me. Whatever it was, I wanted it. Let me tell you"—he chuckled—"I freaked out when I heard it wasn't something you smoke or eat!"

The rest of Saturday night for me was one long headache. Around midnight the complaints became louder and more frequent. In response, the trainer finally asked people to raise their hands if they had any kind of ache or pain. Over half the hands in the room went up. He picked one trainee to come up front for a demonstration.

What followed was a rather incredible exercise in taking responsibility for your own experience of your body. Based on the notion we'd already looked at in relation to our life situations, which is that resistance only makes things continue, the technique we were now shown was a way for us to go deeper into our pain, to experience it totally. Miraculously, the pain disappeared. The technique assists you to experience the pain fully—for example, a backache or headache, by experiencing very specifically its color, size, shape, and how much liquid it would hold if it were a container. For me it has become an invaluable tool in both my life and my practice. (Although est tells people with medical problems to see a physician, several trainees told me that they had gotten rid of medical problems during the training.)

We were finally released to return to beds and bathrooms in the wee hours of the morning. Tucked into our psyches were a couple of other throwaway techniques to blow our belief systems. One that I found incredibly effective was to tell myself just before sleep to wake up on time alive, alert, and refreshed. The next morning, on four hours of sleep, I felt terrific.

When I had hauled my exhausted body out of the hotel that first night, I had felt that I wanted to get as far away from est as I could. I had a backache; I was tired; I was bored; I was also, surprisingly, anxious. I resented everything and everyone connected with est, and especially the trainer for holding a mirror up to my act and not letting me forget my agreements. Was more of the same all I was going to get for my $250? I had a sinking feeling that the whole thing was an enormous fraud. I finally fell asleep more curious than furious. The next morning, though I felt better, I was soon outdoing Lewis Carroll's White Queen; I had 5,000 impossible thoughts before breakfast. And, again, I went off to "transform" my life.

Having taken the time for a second cup of coffee, I arrived at the training a few minutes after nine. My greeting was a stern reminder that I was late. "Who is responsible for your having broken your agreement?" the training assistant asked, as he stood, arms folded, in front of the door into the training. I was, I told him, and dutifully recited out loud, "I acknowledge that I broke my agreement."

One woman among the latecomers refused to take responsibility for her lateness. She argued and cajoled but, of course, got no sympathy and no agreement with her position. All she got, over and over, was the question, "Are you willing to take responsibility for breaking your agreement?" Eventually she realized that her whole life had been based on breaking agreements and refusing to acknowledge that she had. Sobbing as though her heart had broken, she finally capitulated and was allowed into the room.

I was impressed, again, at how each element of the training was directly related to the way each of us leads his life. Even people's excuses for *not* taking the training were the same excuses that kept their lives from working.

The second training day began with sharing. A man in his mid-forties dressed, anachronistically, in a gray suit, white shirt, and blue tie, *got* that he had become a college professor so that he could put everyone down the way he felt they had put him down. "I simply had to prove I was right and they—my parents, everybody—were wrong. Now I know I'm a phony. I don't really know anything."

A woman got up to confess that she had once been raped. She had been out with a man she had picked up at a bar. At the end of the evening, she invited him back to her apartment. It was there he raped her.

Stewart prodded and questioned her mercilessly. She finally got that her identity had become "rape victim." She had made it the primary event in her life, and had talked about it to anyone who would listen, endlessly. And she got that playing "rape victim" wasn't a winning game.

A sophisticated-looking businessman took the microphone to announce that he thought the training was a rip-off. "I don't think you people know what you're doing," he said, "and unless things change soon I'm not going to stay here much longer." "Thank you," Stewart responded. "I acknowledge I heard you." The man remained standing as though waiting for something more and finally sat down only after he was asked to surrender the microphone to a volunteer.

Stewart's responses were becoming predictably familiar, but I never got a sense that they were by rote. When he said, "Thank you. I got it," that meant he didn't agree or disagree with the trainee; he had just listened carefully to the communication and let the trainee know that the communication had been received.

A young schoolteacher admitted, haltingly, that he wished he could love someone but he couldn't. By now the trainees were beginning to see the rackets people run. A loud groan ran through the room.

The trainer launched into a diatribe about love. "I know what love is to you jerks," he barked. "I don't call you on your bullshit and you don't call me on mine. We don't talk about love to assholes who don't know who they are. When you know who you are, then we will talk about love."

I snapped to attention. How many times, I thought, had I believed I was in love only to find that when the going got rough I wanted out. My idea of love was lots of terrific sex and a civilized, undemanding friendship.

"Not being able to love is your racket," bellowed the trainer. "If you want to know who you *were,* keep up your old patterns. If you want to know who you *are,* give up your old patterns."

The training "genius" then stood up. I've heard that there's one in every training—a sophisticated, bright, well-read intellectual who has usually done both therapy and some of the Eastern disciplines and is still seeking the way. "I know all this data you're putting out," he announced. The trainer told him he was "possibly the biggest asshole in the whole room." If he knew so much, Stewart wanted to know, how come he didn't act that way? "What are you hiding? What is happening to you *right now?*"

Trembling, suddenly not so sure of himself, he shared that he felt he was superior to other people, that his interest and knowledge set him apart.

I spoke to him later because I was interested in what he had been into and how he felt about est. "There was nothing wrong in my search," he told me. "It was my attachment to being special on the path that upset me here. The trainer was giving out this special stuff to everyone. I didn't like *not* being different."

An overweight computer programmer shared that he had been in therapy for ten years and that now, for the first time, he felt that he didn't need it anymore. He had clung, he said, to the fact that his mother was a horrible mother, a hang-up that had destroyed every relationship he'd ever had with a woman. "I'm going to call my therapist tomorrow and tell him good-bye," he announced. "I don't need him, because I'm not clinging to that belief anymore."

I shared only once. A Gestalt therapist tried to provoke the trainer into an argument. He declaimed interminably about how est was wrong telling us we were causing all our experiences. Stewart let him talk on and on, and then finally asked him to sit down. He refused. Stewart told him that if he wouldn't sit down, he would have to call a policeman. The confused psychologist still wouldn't budge. Eventually he gave up and turned in his microphone.

I was both ashamed and angry. I stood up to say that all therapists were not like the one who had just spoken. The trainer asked me if I knew what I was doing. I did, I told him. I admitted that I love to make a fuss and blow off my anger by getting angry at something I "believe" in. It was a beautiful opportunity for me. I could put another person down, get sympathy from the rest of the group and unleash some of my excess anger. I had a good time. And I knew, also, that I was running my racket.

The day droned on. It was exquisitely boring. It was like the meditation called in Zen "just sitting." *And* "just sitting" may release hidden inner volcanos. Dr. Charles Tart, psychologist, author of *Altered States of Consciousness,* and Professor at the University of California at Davis, often refers in his lectures to this kind of situation as being the precedent to a disruptive patterning that must necessarily precede a transformation of consciousness.

Late Sunday evening we finally got to one of the major events of the training, the Truth Process. The day before we had been told to pick an "item," something that had been bothering us: a problem, a feeling, a situation we weren't handling. I picked my anger at my friend and lover of the past eight years. I periodically became uncontrollably angry at him; although I understood all the "reasons," knowing them hadn't changed anything.

Two hundred and fifty of us stretched out on the floor to begin the process. The trainer gave us specific instructions. "Locate a space in your right foot," he began, and then he went through the entire body, bringing us to a state of deep relaxation, allowing us to become more aware of ourselves. He then read us a very beautiful poem, written by Werner, based on the writings of the psychologist Abraham Maslow, in which we heard that we are perfect and good, that we can be positive and full of love, and that we can experience good things in our lives.

Stewart's prediction, "You are going to feel every feeling there is to feel," was about to happen.

His directions continued, and the scene grew noisy; an incredible cacophony of sound erupted as each one of the two hundred and fifty men and women, lying flat on their backs on the floor of the giant ballroom, went into their "item." Two hundred and fifty people in every form of emotion, giving free vent to vomiting, shaking, sobbing, hysterical laughing, raging—re-creating experiences in a safe space. No one paid the slightest attention to anyone else. Each person there was concentrating wholly on his own mind/body experience.

In all my years in analysis and through all the other disciplines in which I had received training or treatment, I had never before gotten in touch with the feelings of the incident that came to me in that process.

I was a little girl of nine. I could see myself taunting my father. Furious, he chased me to the bathroom. I ran into it and slammed the door in his face. In the process, I could see him, wild and out of control, trying to push the door in. "You can't catch me," I screamed. At that moment, I felt the tingling in my fingers and the throbbing of my heart that I had experienced when pushing the door shut so many years before. For the first time, I felt "physically" how I had actually separated myself from men by putting a locked door between us, and at that moment I was overcome with feelings of my own goodness and beauty. It was like nothing I had ever experienced before.

The feeling released in that one incident has had continuing and profound effects on me. I can still feel myself responding in anger when my buttons are pushed. But the dimension and the force of the anger have changed. For the first time I feel that I can actually be at its cause, and not at its effect.

At the end of the process we were asked to return to a beach of our own creation. It was to become a place I loved to go to in the processes. Some people experienced it as a place of tranquillity and beauty. Others, like a good friend of mine, turned it into a setting for further drama.

On one occasion she vividly saw a figure she identified as death walking toward her, its arms outstretched in supplication. She backed away, frightened but not repulsed. Then she saw a beautiful and loving man coming toward her from the horizon. She was torn. Finally she threw a kiss to "death" and gently told it that she chose to opt for life. She and the man were united.

When we talked about this incredible fantasy my friend told me that she felt deeply liberated by it. She had the sense that it marked an end and a new beginning in her life.

Sunday night included the much-discussed Danger Process. The room was rearranged into eight parallel rows from which, one row at a time, we filed to the stage to confront—and be confronted by—the audience. As we stood there the trainer exhorted us to "be yourself with people . . . just be with people . . . get what it's like to be with people for the first time in your lives . . . be yourself . . . be who you really are . . . be yourself with people."

I awaited my turn coolly, in contrast to the anguish and agony it evoked in those who preceded me. At other times and in other places (especially at Arica), I had had long, unflinching eye-to-eye contact with people.

When my row moved up front and I looked out on the mass of faces looking right back at me, my back ached but I felt more at ease than I would have dreamed possible. Thus, I was really surprised when a woman next to me fainted, and a man a few steps away began to cry uncontrollably. Later a number of people shared how liberating the anguish they had experienced was. On my way home that night I felt amazingly refreshed.

BETWEEN THE WEEKENDS

The mid-training the following Wednesday evening saw us all reunited like long-lost relatives. Although I had left the training high the previous Sunday, the few days since then had been singularly unremarkable. Not so for most of the others. One by one they got up to share the miracles they had experienced since the weekend.

One man had settled a long-standing hassle with the telephone company. Another had seen his parents for the first time in twelve years. A woman had returned to her husband. Another had had a long-overdue confrontation with her boss. People were needing less sleep, less food, and getting along without painkillers.

There were also more broken agreements. A confessed "pothead" had gotten stoned and experienced total disorientation. A woman had gone on an eating binge which, although not specifically forbidden in the ground rules, was her way of "going unconscious."

An elderly artist complained bitterly that he hadn't been able to sleep, eat, or move his bowels since the training began. "It's unendurable," he said. Later I asked him if he would return to the training the following weekend. "Are you kidding?" he asked. "Leaving now would be like getting off the operating table during mid-surgery."

Before we left, we had a process. I went on an incredible cosmic journey that began over Manhattan and ended at the end of the universe. But I went home depressed. It wasn't enough of a miracle for me.

GETTING IT

The second weekend began, again, with sharing. I was in a foul mood born of disappointment.

Early in the day the trainer reminded us that what we get from the training is nothing. "The problem," he told us, "is that you think nothing is something." Then how come, a woman wanted to know, it takes sixty hours? "Because," he told her, "you have to move through all the somethings you're stuck with to get to nothing."

"To get nothing," he explained, "you have to *get* what you've got and that your life is the way it is." I was confused and getting tired of what I saw as nothing. I desperately wanted something, preferably a break.

The day stretched out interminably. We were coming into the homestretch. The final weekend, we were told, was 85 percent of the training. The data was coming fast and furious now. We had moved from belief systems to very complex material relating to knowledge and reality. On Sunday, we would do "The Anatomy of the Mind," which was what everything was leading up to. In that process we would grasp—and ultimately experience—the nature of mind. (This experience is the foundation for the entire est epistemology.) It was heavy stuff. It would jolt a lot of our cherished beliefs about man, the nature of man, the mind, and the universe.

Adam Smith, in *Powers of Mind,** compares the est training to Samuel Beckett's *Waiting for Godot,* which I had seen many years before. In the play two old tramps wait by a tree on a road for Godot, who doesn't come. One of them says, "Nothing happens, nobody comes, nobody goes, it's awful." Recently when I read Smith's discussion of the play in relation to his experience of est, I found myself nodding in agreement. I, too, had spent the training waiting for nothing to happen and nobody to come. I was suddenly able to recall the play vividly. And *get* it.

* New York: Random House, 1975.

Later that same day I had an extraordinary clear flash of my mother. I saw her in a housedress in the kitchen of my childhood home admonishing me in Latin to do something. I listened carefully and heard her say familiar words, *"Carpe diem,* Adelaide. Seize the day; do it now!"

My mother was a frustrated intellectual who often told me that it was important to *do* rather than just *be.* I had bought it. Now, many, many years later, I was able to respond to her words in my own way. I was "seizing the day." I was discovering, in the est training, who I really was. I was beginning to experience aliveness!

Sunday was when we *got* it. And graduated.

"I'll tell you everything there is to know about life," the trainer said on that final day. "What is, is, and what ain't, ain't.

"Enlightenment," he continued, "is knowing you are a machine. *You are a machine!"* He paused to let that sink in. "You thought"—he glared at us—"that the heavens would part and there would be visitations of angels. That ain't so. You're machines, machines, machines. Whether you accept this or not, it's so."

I chuckled to myself. What a put-on, I thought, and how clever. I waited to hear what *getting it* was really about. Along with at least half of the trainees. Hands began to wave frantically.

"I don't get it," the first protester announced.

"Good," came the reply. "There's nothing to get, so you got it."

From someone else, angrily, "Then why are we here?"

"No special reason," Stewart answered calmly, unconcerned with the growing uproar. People began to laugh, some with recognition, some with anxiety. Some muttered an assortment of obscenities under their breath. The normally quiet room suddenly became alive with chatter. People felt angry, confused, betrayed, disappointed, incredulous.

"I get it," one man volunteered. "Getting it is whatever you get." "If that's what you got," came the response.

Some of the trainees got realizations about concrete things

such as that they wanted a divorce, or to make a relationship work better. Or that they had blamed others for the way they were. Or that they had created their own backaches, migraines, asthma, ulcers, and other ailments.

(The remission of physical ailments is not surprising if one accepts, as many physicians do these days, that mind and body are one and that illness doesn't just *happen* to us. It was remarkable to watch person after person get up and admit that they and they alone were responsible for their physical ailments. Once these people faced the experiences of their lives honestly, their ailments vanished.)

The trainer then asked those of us who were absolutely certain that we didn't get it to stand up. I wasn't sure whether I had or hadn't so I stood up. He then went from one to another of us to find out what we were experiencing.

"Nothing," I told him. "And cheated." "Fine," he responded, "you got it." "How come," I persisted, "I feel rotten when everyone else seems to feel good?" To which he answered, "That's the way you feel. Rotten." He smiled at me. "Take what you get!"

Eventually I did get it. It was just the way he said it would be. I was "enlightened."

My very last experience—at 3:00 A.M. and as part of the graduation ritual—was to do an est "personality profile." Each of us was told certain data about a person known by one of the attending graduates but absent from the training room. We then went into our "space" and from that place described aspects of that person's personality. I was accurate except on one minor detail. Others without any previous experience had the same kind of incredible accuracy.

The way est describes what happens in this process is that people have abilities that were previously considered impossible. "The ability to do personality profiles isn't something that's learned," est explains. "It's something that is uncovered as the result of the training. What is uncovered is the essence of your ability to communicate. When most of us look at people, we really don't see what's there—we see our idea of what's there . . .

our picture of what's there. . . . The personality profile is one centered individual experiencing life through the eyes of another and getting what's really so for him. *It's called communication."*

We finally graduated early Monday morning to the applause of over a hundred prior graduates and with a handshake and good wishes from the trainer. His parting words were: "If you want your life to work, make it work. If you fuck it up, you fuck it up." I got that, too.

AFTERWARD

I hauled my exhausted body and soul back to my hotel room at 4:30 A.M. The tattered brocade drapes and the peeling paint of the once-elegant hotel seemed to mock me, but I didn't care. I turned the light on in the bathroom and a huge black cockroach scurried across the floor. Incredibly, I knew that I had created the experience of the cockroach being there; I had bet a couple of friends there were roaches in that hotel, and now it was fact! What was even more incredible was that I felt benign toward it; it existed, and so did I.

The following morning my train back to Philadelphia got stuck for an hour in the tunnel under the Hudson River. When the conductor announced the delay, I observed passenger reactions. Instead of dealing with the reality that the train was stopped, most of them went into panic behavior. One overweight man became hysterical about being delayed for an appointment. Another took off for the bar. A third went to sleep. They seemed to me to be responses out of each of their belief systems. It struck me as a microcosm of how most of us respond to life; like machines, for every button pushed, we have a predictable reaction.

THE POST-TRAINING

It wasn't until I went to the post-training several days later that I began to see how deeply est had affected—and would continue to affect—my life.

It was like a rehash of a weekend party. I've attended a few other post-trainings in the service of this book and they're remarkably alike wherever they're held. There's a feeling of being among dear friends and of belongingness. It's not unlike a reunion of an encounter group or college class—we had all experienced similar input. The significant difference, however, is the absence of judgments. One person's experience is as valid as another's. This willingness to acknowledge and accept where another person is at is probably why many est graduates make long-time friendships among fellow trainees. (I've also heard from women friends that it's a terrific place to meet eligible men.)

The kind of enthusiasm est graduates share at a post-training is exemplified by singer John Denver's dedication on his *Back Home Again* album. "My purpose in performing is to communicate the joy I experience in living," he's written on the inside jacket. "It is the aliveness already within you that my music is intended to reach. Participating in est has created an amazing amount of space for joy and aliveness in my life. It pleases me to share est with you."

My own post-training, if not as lyrical, was equally eulogistic.

An elderly man who had experienced tremendous withholding through most of the training and then cried his eyes out on the final day (I cried along with him) shared that he had been in this world for over seventy years and had only just now begun to live. Because he was living with his full being, he told us, he no longer feared death.

A woman in her mid-thirties who had looked mousy and frightened when she began the training now looked beautiful and radiant. "I want to share that my asthma, which I've had since I was ten years old, has simply disappeared." Other shared remissions, sounding like Lourdes cures, included two migraine headaches, bladder weakness, and a chronic lower-back pain.

"I want to share that my husband and I have stopped arguing for the first time in three years," a stunning young woman told us. "He can't understand it and neither can I."

The trainer responded by telling her to "just experience it. You don't have to do anything else."

An eighteen-year-old girl shared that she had had a visionary experience since the training. A businessman said he managed better. A textile designer said her designs were more creative.

One by one, over a couple of hours, people spoke about changes big and little that had taken place in their lives. Many had cleared up misunderstandings, others had cleaned their houses, others had resolved money situations, and others found themselves getting up on time and starting their days with enthusiasm. A few were meditating better, some gave up jobs or began new ones, and some reported communicating with parents or children for the first time in their lives.

There were unhappy experiences as well. An actress told us that she had been "scared shitless." She was having constant headaches and felt more confused than ever. "I don't know why I chose this when it hurts so much. I don't know where I am." The trainer advised her to stay with it. "You see," he explained, "if all you got was nothing, just experience that. That's all there is."

A young man announced that the day after the training he had been fired from his job. "I experienced how guilty my boss felt and I said, comforting him, that it was really O.K. That night, after I phoned a few people to tell them and told everyone not to feel sorry for me, that I was responsible for it, I went out for a drink and helped a friend in trouble. I feel great," he added.

One woman lethargically told us that she had been deeply depressed. "Experience your barrier of depression," she was told. "Just be there with it."

Valerie Harper, star of the TV series *Rhoda* and four-time Emmy Award winner, shared her experience with the *New Age Journal* (September, 1975). After taking est, she told them, "almost all the effort has gone out of my life. I used to be in constant tension—I would struggle, strain and sweat to make things happen. Since I took the training, I've suddenly seen all the tension and the working-at-things, and I'm giving it up!"

She reported that experience of her work had been transformed, that although she still got angry and impatient, she no longer was at the mercy of her emotions, and that all her relationships have changed. "I used to be really resistant to becoming a star— I never accepted my fame. Now I'm beginning to enjoy it."

In order to give everyone the chance in the post-training to share what they got, two minutes were allotted for each of us to talk with his neighbor. A handsome, well-dressed rancher from Wyoming told me that this had been his first consciousness trip of any kind. He wasn't searching for anything, he said, but his business hadn't been doing so well, and since he had to be in New York for something else, he decided to take the training.

"I'm more clear now that I'm the boss," he said, "and what I say goes. I've been pussyfooting with a particular guy and it just doesn't work. Otherwise"—he shrugged—"I don't know. I'll just go with it and see what happens."

est says that what happens as a result of the training depends entirely upon the individual. There are no guarantees, est tells you. You take what you get.

About two months after my training I was at San Francisco's St. Francis Hotel and found myself in an elevator that was all glass on one side. I had been in glass elevators before, and they had always sent me into a panic. I would close my eyes and of course miss the spectacular view.

This time when I felt the surge of panic in my stomach, I experienced it fully, and then observed it disappear instantly. I opened my eyes to enjoy the magnificent view of the San Francisco hills against a golden sunset. I had stood my ground and won.

In many ways the est training has intensified my awareness that I run my own show, whatever I choose it to be. I do that by being in my life right now instead of yesterday, last month, when I was five, when I'll be sixty-five. Life is only what it is. Not the way it used to be or ought to be or might be.

My favorite Werner aphorism sums it up beautifully: "If God told you exactly what it was you were to do, you would be happy doing it no matter what it was. What you're doing is what God wants you to do. Be happy."

Margot

◆───────◆

Margot, thirty-eight, is an intensely alive, divorced mother of two. She is an editor and writer.

I decided to take the est training because I thought it would be a hot subject for a magazine piece. I wouldn't admit to myself that I really was interested in the training for myself.

I went into it feeling pretty armored against it. I had done a lot of therapy—group, encounter, individual, bioenergetics, primal—after I was divorced, and finally gave it up because I felt I was reinforcing the unhealthy, dependent part of me. I liked the idea that est rejected people they described as "losing" in therapy. I was tired of being a loser.

I found the training agonizing. In fact, I hated it. I cried a lot and got in touch with a lot of stuff I had never experienced before. Even so, when I finished it I was disappointed. I don't know what I had expected but I wasn't willing to "take what I got."

The most powerful thing that happened to me during the training was that I completed [ended] two incomplete relationships that were messing up the rest of my life.

In one of the processes my ex-husband and his bride-to-be came into my center and we had an incredible talk about their wedding and what it meant to them and me. It was very beautiful and very real. Afterward I was able to accept their marriage and give up all the negative stuff I had invested in it. I really wished them well. And I got that I was doing with my life exactly what I wanted to be doing and especially that I was not currently in a relationship out of choice. I still had things to clean up in my life before I could have the kind of relationship I wanted.

In another process I finally ended a relationship that had

actually ended more than two years before. A part of me was still clinging to the hope that we could get back together. I had loved him. And I had rejected him. Now I saw that holding on to this illusion kept me from moving on.

After the training I felt smug that it hadn't turned my life around, as it had promised to do. I was damned if I would be just like all the other thousands who came out of est singing its praises and attributing to it all kinds of miraculous breakthroughs. Whatever might happen to me, I told myself, would just be more of the same—a few new openings, a few new interesting experiences, another baby step closer to wholeness.

Despite my resistance, though, my life became very intense after the training. Two weeks later I had an incredible gut re-experience of my father and myself when I was a little girl. I suddenly knew that he had really loved me. Because he's often disconnected from his feelings, I have chosen to see him as incapable of love. In fact, since my teens I had totally rejected his love. From that I saw that I ultimately rejected every man who had ever loved or been loved by me. I cried from the depths of my soul.

Some terrific stuff is also happening with my kids. They're taking a lot more responsibility for what goes on in their lives and dumping on me a lot less, which of course gives me space to dump on them a lot less, which is letting us all feel a lot more love for each other. My ten-year-old son got into trouble in school the other day and then came home and told me that he had created it. Because I've been very wrapped up in a project the last couple of weeks, my eight-year-old daughter announced last night that, instead of waiting for me to be finished, she was going to take responsibility for making her own birthday party.

I don't like to give est credit for any of this. I distrust Werner and other things about the organization. But I have to admit that it works. Or at least it's working for me.

5

Volunteering and
Vomit Bags

"The purpose of assisting is to assist."
—*Werner Erhard*

I stood on the aisle with a pile of vomit bags in my arms. I had no idea what time it was; it could have been anywhere from late afternoon to midnight. My legs ached. My head was pounding. What I wanted more than anything else was to be prone with a cold drink at my fingertips and surrounded by the sweet smell of home.

Instead, I had been standing in the same place for twenty minutes, my eyes scanning the couple of dozen trainees assigned to me, watching for someone's hand to shoot into the air signaling that he wanted to vomit. So far I had had three takers. As I waited for more, I concluded that the consciousness movement had erupted, literally and figuratively.

I was a volunteer at an est training. I had decided to volunteer for the two weekends because I wanted to see what it was like from the other side.

The est volunteer experience is regarded by est as a microcosm of life on the "outside." I wanted to know first-hand what that meant. When I had inquired about assisting a few weeks earlier, an est assistant had told me, "Everything you will do will give you an opportunity to see where you are coming from, what your machine is up to."

The rhythm of the volunteer day began at 6:30 A.M. to allow enough time to set up for the trainees arriving a couple of hours later. My first assignment was to go out for coffee: two with, one without, one with sugar on the side. I was just short of devastated. I had hoped to be in the "big" room, observing and participating in the training, being important. But after the coffee errand other things were to have priority.

My next task was to arrange the name tags. They had to be ten in a vertical row, not touching, in perfect parallel columns. I was already aware of est's policy regarding name tags; everyone wore them at all times. Now I was to become aware of est's meticulous attention to detail. The instructions for each chore were exact, delivered with the precision one would expect from an excellent instruction manual. I was expected to carry out the chore with the same precision.

From name tags I went to tablecloths. My assignment was to cover several long, rectangular tables with tablecloths. My instructions: each tablecloth was to be pinned with a square corner (fortunately I had learned how in girl scout camp) and should almost but not quite touch the floor. Another mindless task. While I went through the motions I eavesdropped on a conversation a few feet away. A mistake.

I looked up to see the person supervising the assistants standing alongside me. Confronting me with the directness characteristic of est-ers (a graduate can be known by his direct eye contact), he kindly but firmly instructed me to do the tablecloth over. "It touches the floor," he explained with a solemnity that from someone else would have indicated a critical error in a major undertaking. But there was no cruelty, no satisfaction, no judgment in his statement. It simply was.

I redid the tablecloth with my full attention. My square corners were perfect and the cloth hung to precisely the right length. I had completed the job, which in est terms meant I had finished it with nothing left out of the experience and I could move on to something else.

I had an unexpected but interesting reaction to all of this. When I stood away from the table to observe my efforts, I felt satisfaction. Not anger, as I might have expected for having had to do the job over, but pleasure in a job completed and well done.

In completing this task, I got an important aspect of the est business. The attention to detail that had so irritated me was, in fact, a significant factor in est's success. Werner had brought from his management-training days his experience that little things done correctly make big things work better. I was beginning to accept that. Which made my next assignment only slightly more palatable.

From tablecloths I graduated to chairs, one of the more important but also one of the most inane of the volunteer responsibilities. These jobs were all described as "supporting the space," that is, creating an efficient and comfortable environment so the trainees can give their undivided attention to the training.

Doing chairs meant arranging 250 chairs in an exact, prescribed order. So exact must the alignment into rows and sections be that the first time around we redid it four times until we got it right. "Right" meant that a piece of string pulled taut from one end of a row to the other never curved.

My involvement with chairs over the two weekends was relentless. I aligned them, rearranged them, took them away, brought them back. A fellow volunteer dubbed the total experience "the chair training." Around the third or fourth time I did chairs, I had a realization.

Contemporary man, with all his senses intact, often acts as though he were deaf, dumb, and blind. Because there are too many messages being beamed at him—and too many of them are painful—he has chosen to be half alive instead of fully alive. He dreams and worries about the future. He frets about or retreats to the past. He rarely gives his total self to the here and now of the present.

For me, the intense focus on the now in my volunteer experience was at first unpleasant, unfulfilling, unproductive, un-just-about-everything. When I committed myself to it, it was satisfying. Doing chairs, I really *got* that the only thing that matters is the moment. You cannot be involved only in good moments and not be involved in those moments you don't like. Feeling alive is experiencing every moment—pleasant and unpleasant.

I was reminded of a classic Zen aphorism. If what one does before the Tao ("the Way") is to chop wood and drink water, then what does one do *after* the Tao? The answer: chop wood and drink water.

It was around this time that I found myself really enjoying my work. I eagerly accepted my reassignment from chairs to bathrooms. What truths could I discover, I wondered, in a search for the shortest route from the training room to the toilets?

This enthusiasm, however, waxed and waned. There were times when I felt a grimness about it all. Except when we were instructed to smile in the role of "greeter," we were to remain poker-faced. When I remarked on this to my supervisor, he said, simply, "The purpose of assisting is to assist. Do what you're doing now. Do your *humor* at humor time."

About midway through the first weekend, I became concerned that I might never get into *the* room, which had been my primary goal in volunteering. I complained to the person to whom I was responsible. He eye-balled me for a moment and then said, kindly, "And you may *never* get in the room."

Because I generally make my needs known "upfront," I'm accustomed to getting my way in most things. I also don't accept "no" easily. Somehow, this time was different. I accepted what he said. No rebellion, no demands, no complaints. Instead, I took responsibility for my intention to be in the training room. And, of course, it happened.

A few weeks later, when I visited est headquarters in San Francisco, I spoke with volunteers who had worked directly with or around Werner. I wondered how much more or less rigorous his expectations were in comparison to those of my own supervisors.

A young woman who had volunteered to clean the San Francisco town house where Werner has his office told me that she had been instructed in detail about how to do the job. "I had to clean under each object, such as those on a coffee table, and then replace it precisely where I found it, not a half-inch away." (All housekeeping functions are now performed by paid personnel.)

The person assigned to clean toilets at headquarters that day reported that there was one, and only one, est way to do the job. He shared that he had been astonished to discover how much thought and effort could go into cleaning toilets the est way: i.e., completely.

And one of the est office staff confessed that Werner can become very loud when a job isn't completed. "I quake, but I know he loves me. Does that sound really crazy? That's the way it is and so you go about your job the way Werner wants the job done."

Several est workers proudly told me that est graduates were in great demand on the California job market. A number of businesses, in fact, were reported to be hiring only est-ers.

Subsequently I met the manager of a charming restaurant on Fisherman's Wharf who told me that most of his staff were est people and that, whenever an old-timer left, he would be replaced by an est-er regardless of whether or not he or she had ever done that kind of work before.

His reason, this conscientious and able man told me, was that est grads "don't stand around waiting for someone else to do their work, or to be told what needs to be done. They don't whine and complain that anything is too much for them or that a particular job is beyond their job description. They do their jobs well and cheerfully."

Incredible! It occurred to me that if Werner actualized his proposal to train millions, it might have a dramatic effect on everyone's job performance.

Being an est volunteer made me very conscious of what making and breaking agreements in the est sense was all about. In a society where "rules are made to be broken," it was refreshing—if at times disconcerting—to experience est's insistence on fulfilling agreements.

A case in point occurred on the first day of the training. A man I estimated to be in his middle forties, successful, sure of himself, had flown up from Florida the evening before to take the training. He was obviously excited about this commitment and presented himself to us with pleased expectation written on his face.

At the registration table he was asked if he had brought a letter from his therapist giving permission for him to take the training. This was a requirement because he had answered affirmatively to a question on the application form that asked if he had ever been hospitalized for psychiatric care or a mental disorder. Because he had forgotten or thought it irrelevant, he hadn't gotten the letter. Although he had been hospitalized twenty-five years previously, and despite his long and costly trip, he was told that he would not be allowed to take the training.

He screamed and pounded on the table and threatened dire consequences and paced the floor. But the decision, confirmed after a call to California, remained no. I watched him leave, rejected and dejected, suitcase in hand, and wondered if he'd be back. Would I? I asked myself. I wasn't sure that I would have.

One of the most striking things about being an est volunteer was the chance it gave me to observe at close hand, and to be a part of, the est community.

I saw that Werner has created a situation where people clamor to volunteer.* It saves the cost of thousands of salaries and it provides est with dedicated people to attend to the myriad details (chair arranging, bathroom maps) that contribute to est's success. Werner told me that what people really want to do with their lives is to make a contribution to the well-being of others. He said that people who experience themselves find that purpose within themselves.

The basis of the volunteer program is that it is a real-life after-training workshop in which you get to experience responsibility along with other est graduates. A free post-graduate course, in effect. Volunteers repeatedly told me that they felt they got more from their work than est got from their services.

* est says that 6,000 to 7,000 graduates work as volunteers in the course of a year.

It was certainly true of my own experience. I later learned that it is a requirement of the assistants program that people remain in it only as long as they get at least as much value from assisting as they contribute.

The est volunteer experience is also a pleasurable and fulfilling one for most. One can't be around est offices and events without noticing that everyone seems intensely involved. The offices have a softly humming and confident busyness.

Everyone—and this includes old pros as well as first-timers—seems to be "on purpose," which is an est term for getting the job done. Although nothing is supposed to interfere with the task at hand, Werner has told staff members, "This is not a war. In doing our job in est, we are not to think in terms of allowable levels of casualties. Each individual is to be respected and no individual may be sacrificed for any reason." Quite impressive and quite different from the offices I've worked in.

My feelings about this aspect of est, the sense of community and eager commitment, is that it fulfills a deep need in contemporary American society. Critics of est have compared it, disparagingly, with old-time religion. If one defines religion as a belief system, then est would not qualify as a religion. (When the question was actually posed to a trainer during a seminar, in classic est-ian fashion the response was, "I got it. It's not and if that's what you experience it's O.K.")

What est does have in common with traditional Western religion is its sense of service, of mission, and of course its definition of a way of being and experiencing. And, like many religions, est has its own language. Not only does this language provide a unique way of communicating, it also immediately identifies whoever uses est phrases as an ex-asshole, a member of the club.

This experience of belonging—in a special place, with a particular group of people—was once provided by one's church. Today an est graduate might put in long hours of painstaking work and have such an experience—a sense of belonging, of serving. I've seen a similar kind of fervor among volunteer workers in a political campaign. The difference between the est and the political volunteer experience is that est-ers experience satisfaction in their lives and activists can merely *hope* that their efforts will change their lives.

An interesting aside is that for a while there was a rule against sex between est staff members. To the relief of all who mentioned it to me, that rule has been rescinded.

Working at est means instant friends, confidants, and people who sincerely are interested in one another. Several times when I was at an est office someone would burst into tears and immediately find both a sympathetic ear and assistance in *getting* whatever the tears related to. The problems shared were intimate ones—a bad trip with parents, a lover, a boss. Nothing seemed too private, too embarrassing, too crazy to hide. Time and time again I was struck by the contrast between an interchange among est grads and the comparative superficiality of communication between friends and colleagues on the outside. If the former sometimes made me uncomfortable, ultimately it was far more satisfying than the latter.

What did I get from the intense experience of being an est volunteer?

The high point of the weekend came when the man in charge of logistics said to me, after I had mapped the shortest and most efficient route to the bathrooms, "Thank you, Adelaide. You have done an excellent job in writing these instructions." Wow! I was high for hours. From which I *got* that it's a lot more satisfying to be *on purpose* than scattered, *and* that I enjoy someone else's approval for "a job well done." I also *got* that both my intention and my attention determined the quality of my work.

As for my understanding of the est operation, I finally *got* why the est organization is so successful. The value of its philosophy and techniques is only part of the picture. The rest comes from the fact that people give their best efforts to est, that out of the intense focus, discipline, and caring of staff and volunteers has come an incredibly tight, efficient, and effective business.

Each est volunteer "gets off" on doing his job, be it toilet-cleaning or supervising, when his work is completed. Multiply one worker's experience several thousand times and you get several thousand super-efficient, happy, and devoted workers. Free! They not only care about what they do, they bring loving concern to what they do. It works!

Richard M. Dawes, M.D.

Dr. Dawes is Clinical Assistant Professor in the
Department of Psychiatry at Louisiana State
University and is on the Board of Directors of
De Paul Psychiatric Hospital In New Orleans.
He was a general practitioner for twelve years
before he returned to school to become a psychiatrist. He decided to take the est training
after reading Marcia Seligson's article on est,
which first appeared in New Times and was
reprinted in Cosmopolitan. His former wife, his
present wife, and his two children have since
taken the training.

I'm enthusiastic about est because it works. I've seen it work
with myself, my patients, and my friends. I have broken
through so many barriers, for both myself and my patients,
that I can only be high about it. Until now I have always
been a therapeutic nihilist, exploring everything but never
enthusiastic about anything.

In my own life, I have faced many things that have been
uncomfortable. During the Truth Process, I got in touch with
material inaccessible to me during my seven years of analysis, which is a reflection of how intense and effective the est
experience is. I picked depression as my item and I got in
touch with my body feelings of "coldness." I began to shiver.
The picture that came to mind was of me as a little boy of
five on a day when it had actually snowed in New Orleans.
I had packed snow into my pockets to bring home to my
mother and then passed out "cold" on the sidewalk. I experienced a tremendous fear of being alone. It was exceedingly powerful. In all my years on the couch I had never
gotten in touch with that alone feeling. When that process

was over I was so relieved that I laughed uproariously, as did so many others.

I have a twenty-year-old son with whom I have had terrible communication. He had been severely depressed and we were always afraid to talk, to tread on each other. Of course, what we did was to tread on each other. What you resist is what you get, as they say in est. He took the training and our communication is now terrific.

After the training, I took the Communication Workshop, which really put everything together for me. It was a spiritual experience. I realized that I had never communicated in my life. Werner said, "To communicate you have to have absolute admiration and respect. You can't be a brilliant therapist without love, admiration, and respect for the patient." I do love my patients now, regardless of their trips. I experience their experiences and get fulfillment from my work in a way I never thought possible.

Work with my patients has changed since I took est. A teen-ager I had been working with for some time, who was hostile, paranoid, isolated, bitter, and a borderline schizophrenic, was so obnoxious that I really didn't want him as a patient. He's now become someone with whom I'm working very well. I can laugh with him now. I can call him on his tough-guy games. And I've started to work with him to experience his loneliness. While I used to help patients strengthen their defense mechanisms, now I have them experience rather than repress certain patterns and they go away. This same young man, for example, now force-feeds his depression. [In this context, to "force-feed" a depression would be to experience it fully instead of trying to get rid of it by various means.]

A woman patient who had had multiple hospitalizations realized, in the process of being helped, that she was a psychosomatic cripple. Because of my est training the seductive-manipulative aspects of her moaning and complaining became clear to me. When I communicated this to her, she was able to tell me, "If I face my feelings, I'll die." She had never gone that far or been that honest before. She became more alive. When she left the hospital, the staff remarked on how much she had changed.

I see now, also, that there are some patients who don't appreciate and don't want to experience feelings, who would rather have medication or electric shock. Even so, I respect them and acknowledge where they are. And then cut through their games.

I have sent twelve patients from New Orleans to est trainings in New York and San Francisco. I've done that because it works, because it's therapeutic, regardless of their disclaimers that est is not therapy. The training encourages people to work through and experience their barriers and get out of the cognitive mind which dominates so much of our culture.

Out of these twelve patients, three didn't like it—they thought it was atrocious, boring, exhausting. All three had had lots of therapy and were isolated, intellectual people. One week after they were back in therapy with me each one of them cried for the first time in our work together. They got in touch with feelings they had been avoiding for years. Two out of three now acknowledge that they got a lot from the training. The third still denies it was helpful; he, I observed, got the most from it. The other nine sound even more enthusiastic than I do. I find, incidentally, that I communicate better with est graduates than with other people.

There is currently some resistance to est from other psychiatrists in New Orleans. They have heard about it from me and are curious. A colleague who does a group at a hospital where I have individual patients is amazed at the change in my patients, how they are breaking through their barriers. A couple of others, though, are antagonistic because they think Werner is a con artist, or because of his name change.*

It's scary for therapists. They have to feel uncomfortable

* See Chapter 8 for discussion of this.

about something that threatens all their years of training. I, too, was scared that last day of the training. I wondered how I could continue all the stuff I had learned when it didn't mean anything.

I am convinced est offers true transformation. And in an amazingly short period of time.

6

est Goes to Prison

> *"I got that what happened to me ain't no mis-*
> *take. I planned it that way."*
> *—A prisoner in Lompoc's maximum security*
> *section*

"I'm here for bank robbery. It doesn't take too much smarts to walk into a bank and tell them to hand over the money. I kick myself in the ass every time I think about it. I know I got more potential and qualifications than to do something like that. But I was impatient. I wanted it *then*. est brought me a lot of realizations and I guess you could call it waking up."

I was in the office of the psychologist of the Federal Correctional Institution at Lompoc, California, listening to one of the thirteen convicts who would be talking to me about est.

I was there to see for myself what est had done for prisoners; almost every story about Werner Erhard and est had mentioned the prison training. I was there also for a colleague of mine, a psychiatrist who is head of psychiatric services for the city of Philadelphia. I would report to him what I had experienced so that he could consider the value of bringing the training into the city's prison system.

Because of what I *got* from the training about agreements, I was experiencing some guilt. Neither before nor during my visit did I divulge that I was writing this book. The letter requesting my visit had come from my colleague and referred only to that aspect of my investigation which related to his work. (Later I let the people I had met know about the book. The prison psychologist kidded me for not being upfront. "Didn't you get that it would have been O.K. to have walked in here and told the truth?" I didn't then, but I would now.)

The reason I withheld this information was that I wanted to get the real story rather than a public relations fabrication. I felt that admitting the full truth about my visit would prevent me from getting to their truth.

In est terms, my *reasons* were irrelevant. Reasons aren't real; people make them up to justify what they want to do. What mattered was whether I was willing to take responsibility (and the consequences) for what I was doing. I was, which meant that I was prepared to incur the wrath of the authorities, to get tossed out of the prison, to suffer the pangs of guilt, and to face whatever else might result from my half-truth. As I now put this into perspective, it occurs to me that my experience was exactly what the est prison training was all about: taking responsibility for making and breaking agreements.

I flew to Los Angeles and then boarded a Greyhound bus for the four-hour ride through rolling cowboy country to the federal prison. The next morning, after I had spent an anxious night at a nearby motel, a curious cab driver ("No visiting hours on Thursday, ma'am") deposited me before an enormously high fence topped with three strands of barbed wire and a fifty-foot-high glass tower, which were a visitor's welcome. The object of my journey, a huge gray concrete building, loomed before me from across a vast empty plain.

Feeling small and vulnerable, I waited with my driver for an acknowledgment of my presence. It came out of the air, as though from nowhere, with a curt "What do you want?" I identified myself to the faceless voice and after a short wait was allowed through the wire fence, whereupon I identified myself again and was admitted to the reception area.

The intimidating security structures, the bars on every window, the gray tiled corridors—all reminded me of every prison movie I had ever seen. It was both awesome and sobering. If the whole thing smacked of a grade-B jail tale, the climax to my entrance scene was in the best tradition of Hollywood slapstick. Shaken after my solo walk across the flat, empty space between the fence and the building, I asked the receptionist what I could do with my suitcase. He considered the question seriously before suggesting, apologetically, that it would be best to lock it up. "We have a lot of thievery around here," he explained, poker-faced!

Dr. Scott Moss, the mental health coordinator and a charming and knowledgeable man, soon appeared to escort me to the first of my appointments. I was grateful for his presence, especially as we moved through the huge, busy corridor where prisoners and staff walked briskly about their business. It wasn't until after I cleared the third barrier that the full import of what I was up to hit me: If, in fact, sixty hours of est training could transform some of the rapists, murderers, burglars, and other criminals who populated Lompoc, what might that mean for the society at large? Intrigued by the possibilities but skeptical, I decided to just stick close to Dr. Moss and keep my ears and eyes open.

I had fortunately arrived in time to listen in on a series of interviews by two students from San Francisco State University who were doing their masters theses about est at Lompoc.

In the initial encounter, a researcher stated that the investigation was not related to the prison, that the prisoner's name would not be used, and that he should feel free to be as honest as he wanted since nothing would be used for or against him. Each was asked the same questions, which dealt primarily with what he had experienced from the training.

The first, a good-looking young black (all but two of the prisoners I met were black), grinned self-consciously when asked what he thought of the training. "Cool, man, cool. And I *got* that what happened to me ain't no mistake. I planned it that way."

I could barely believe my ears. A ghetto youth assuming full responsibility for his life instead of blaming it all on bad housing, vitamin deficiencies, overcrowded schools, a father who had deserted, no money or jobs or love? It was exactly what I wanted to hear but I mistrusted it. Too glib, I thought; he's getting off on his performance.

But as the men came and went, I heard the same theme over and over. Convicts admitting that they had known what they were getting into and now accepting the consequences.

From another, a young redhead, "When I run up against a brick wall, I know that's the way I want it."

Another, a tough-looking six-footer: "What I see now is that I used my own agreements instead of looking out there at the world. I never bought anyone else's agreement until I got hit over the head, literally, with a club. The sky was the limit in my life. Oh, hell, I'm not going to say I'm perfect now but even here I get along a hell of a lot better than I used to."

Each had come to the training for a different reason. "I took it because there wasn't anything else to do," a twenty-three-year-old blond who looked like a college student explained. "But I really roll with the punches now. Sure I'll be glad when I get out of here [he had three years left on a five-year sentence]. But right now I'm paying attention to right now."

The words sounded pat to me but the person speaking was totally real. Later, others were to say essentially the same thing. If Werner had accomplished nothing else during the trainings, this kind of acceptance alone was worth the whole venture. I was told that most prisoners spent their lives daydreaming about the distant future, looking to the time when they would be released. By being in the here and now, and by accepting that "here" meant three sets of barbed wire, guard towers, and restricted movement, then they had choices. A former dope dealer summed it up with a Werner quote: "It's much easier to ride the horse in the direction he's going."

Some of those interviewed hadn't completed the training. "They had X-rated movies going that weekend," one confessed with a grin. Another, who felt Werner "could make a person change their mind about love," said he got tired of sitting. And another left "because I'm partly satisfied with what I am." The training is heavy stuff, and I could see that an X-rated movie was an easy distraction.

The most interesting responses were from men who were knowledgeable about therapeutic and rehabilitation techniques.

They had been involved in counseling or drug abuse programs and/or group therapy, including Transactional Analysis. Some of these programs they had experienced before they were imprisoned or in other prisons; others they had pursued at Lompoc.

A particularly sharp, articulate graduate told us: "I stood up there and had the most fantastic thought. Everyone looked so . . . transparent. And I suddenly realized, 'What am I afraid of? Them?' I was sick that I've walked around afraid this long. I think about that every time I get into a conversation and our fronts go up and I can feel the fear between us. I don't take the initiative yet to try and break down that fear and to see just how far it would go."

Another observed that the people who don't get anything out of est are the same people who don't get anything out of counseling or therapy. "They just don't want to look at themselves."

When the series of brief interviews was over, I met with Burt Kerish, Lompoc's competent and gracious clinical psychologist for the last fifteen years. He had been in the first Lompoc training, conducted personally by Werner (there have been two trainings so far, attended by 118 prisoners). Eager to share his experience, Burt told me that he *got* that people both in and out of the prison found him intimidating. "And I was not aware of it." Among his life changes since the est training: "I find more aliveness in assisting at est than playing at the beach and I enjoy both."

Burt had asked three est graduates to meet with me in an informal setting to discuss the training in more detail. I was excited about it. One of the three, I was told, had been convicted of rape and bank robbery. Another was also a bank robber, and the third was a big-time dope smuggler. We were sitting around Burt's office, informally, with no bars, guards, or guns—none of the props I had expected.

Of the three men, Jack* was the most eager to share his experience. He was also the most articulate, a handsome young black who had been convicted of both rape and bank robbery.

---

* I've used fictional names for prisoners throughout this chapter.

"What I got out of est is self-control and self-awareness."
His deep brown eyes looked directly at me. "Some days my
mind just can't stop wishing I were out. So then I say, 'Why
wish to be out there when you can't? Just relax and flow with it
and take it as it comes.' I go through that maybe ten times a
day to pull myself out of it. But it works. I tell myself, 'This is
all there is right now so just relax and quit fighting because you
can't do anything but worry yourself to death trying to make it
something it isn't.'"

Jack had been in Transactional Analysis in the prison and he
felt that TA was his first awareness of how he was "put together."† He also felt it had prepared him for the est experience
which he had been through eight months previously. "Frankly,"
he said, "none of it is any magic for me. But what works best is
something I got from est, and that's telling myself that this is
what it is, so just let it be."

He confessed that he had slept during the processes so he
had no recollection of them. (Recall that the trainer claims all
you have to do is be at the training—awake or asleep—and the
rest just happens.)

While Jack and I talked the other two men listened and
watched, saying nothing. But when he began to speak about the
Danger Process, their attention picked up. It was the one process the prisoners I talked with had consistently responded to.

"I got up on the platform," Jack began, "and looked at the
rest of the prisoners and I saw that everybody in that audience
was really scared. While I was watching one guy, especially,
who wouldn't look at nobody—he just stared at the wall—I
thought that it couldn't be that bad. So when I got up there I
just started looking people in the eye. And I saw that they were

† Transactional Analysis is a system developed by the late Dr. Eric
Berne in which the personality is arbitrarily divided into three parts:
parent, adult, and child. A shorthand, rhythmic explanation is that the
"parent" part is concerned with what you were taught; the "adult" with
thought; the "child" with felt. TA is a concrete system for looking at
oneself. It is widely used in therapy and business to help people clarify
their thinking and feelings, and then change their behavior.

scared of me." It was an important realization for this man who had devoted his life to compensating for his fears.

The man they called Smarty finally spoke up. He was thoughtful and chose his words carefully. "I can conceive, now, of not doing what I used to do, on the basis of not breaking my agreements. Both TA and est helped. I have a wife and three kids out there and, if not for that, I would have gone back to my old bag, which is running drugs and making a lot of money, but not now."

Bill, the third prisoner, attacked Smarty for his new views. "You lived before for the accumulation of money through drugs. You going to really change your motivations now?"

"Yes, I am." The answer was soft, honest, undefensive. Bill must have believed him. He didn't press his point.

Instead, he offered to talk about himself. "I put in for parole and they disapproved it. When I found out, I got pretty upset, went back to my cell, and just sat there experiencing my upset. You know what?" He paused for dramatic effect. "It went away!"

"I'm going back to school to get a B.A. in sociology, and maybe become a social worker. I don't want the world. But I'd like to live as comfortably as I can and that's what I'm going to do." He pounded his fist for emphasis. "I just read an article called 'The Americanized Robot' about how people are working and spinning their wheels, and we here are just rejects. Sure, there were a lot of us who were programmed to buck society. But not me anymore." And then, in case I hadn't heard, he repeated, "No more."

Burt Kerish wanted to talk about his experience—which surprised me. The prisoners eagerly absorbed his words. There was no hint of glee on their faces as they heard their superior expose what in other circumstances would be considered weakness. They were with him.

"The first thing I did when I went into the training was to put my psychologist number on it. That was probably the last time. What I do now is simply suspend all judgment. Judgment is a voice in the back of my head and it still goes on but I don't allow it to affect my relationships."

Burt shared that he had always been on guard against being taken in by anybody—car salesmen, insurance salesmen, or "slick Philadelphia cons like Werner. Now what I do is to enjoy him and everybody else while that little voice inside just keeps going.

"I'm eligible to retire soon," he told me. "Until I took est I was just going to play, which meant sailing or sitting. Now I look at play as if it were work and there is no difference. People ask me what the hell I do around here, in the prison, and I tell them I'm playing. No one can tell the difference because I'm having such a good time."

I was deeply moved listening to these four men—three on the inside looking out, and one their mentor, with them as an equal. I had come to the prison expecting to find grim tragedy: people who were bitter, lost, angry. They may have been there, but they weren't among the men I encountered.

Instead what I found were people leading caged lives with integrity. I found people whose lives had gone wrong but who were facing where they were at with humor, intelligence, compassion, and courage.

When it came time for me to leave, I did so reluctantly. I felt that I had found an oasis of beauty and love in the midst of a wasteland. I had made real contact with those I met, and we had shared some good honest experiences. I would cherish those moments always; I got that I enjoyed those hours in prison more than many hours when I'm "having pleasure."

We all shook hands and then, spontaneously, we hugged each other. At the time it seemed the most natural thing to do. It was only later, hours after I had left the prison, that the incongruity of me in the arms of these tough, once-brutal men hit me. I found myself laughing out loud at the recollection.

When I left the prison and heard the electronic lock click shut behind me, I had the fleeting sense that I was being locked *out*.

The est involvement with prisoners is more than an interesting one. I feel that it may have broad ramifications for all of us, from those who park illegally and cheat on their income-tax returns to the big-time gangsters who end up in jail.

The essence of it all is taking responsibility for your behavior. An est article about the prison training says, "Being in prison doesn't seem to be such a terrible punishment for people after they have taken responsibility for their lives. Being responsible may be the key to making prisons work. As Ted [Ted Long, an est trainer] pointed out in the training, 'If you guys find out that you dig it here, they might have to close this place.'"

Take that outside prison walls and what you get is: Being responsible may be the key to making society work. And if everyone finds out they dig being wherever they are, fulfilling their responsibilities in their offices and schools and homes, then society's punitive measures might become obsolete.

Werner tells the story of his experience training a ghetto chief:*

"About half way through the training, Arthur [the chief] stood up and said, 'You know, Werner, I just realized something. You are going to take all my stuff away from me. And if I go back to the ghetto, and I don't have my stuff, I'm liable to get killed. I don't know whether I belong here or not.' Anyway, Arthur took the whole training. . . . The point of the story was, by becoming detached . . . by becoming unattached to his survival mechanism, he became the *cause* of his behavior instead of the *effect* of his behavior."

What, if any, long-term effect does the training have on the prisoners who took it? Burt Kerish, as quoted by an est staff writer, says: "Most of the inmates who took that first training have been released, and I don't mean to say it was because of the training. I don't really know. Some of them got out because their sentences were up. Others were able to tell the parole board clearly that they were ready to be responsible."

The *About est* brochure quotes a letter sent to est by Frank

* *East West Journal* (September, 1974).

Kenton, the recently retired warden of Lompoc: "There has been nothing but praise about the program from those involved and any inmates and staff who have heard about it. Seldom has such a program received such acceptance. We thank you for presenting it here at Lompoc, and the benefits are certainly reflected in the attitudes and many positive responses that have come to our staff's attention."

Most telling, although inconclusive, is the evaluation done by Dr. Scott Moss in July, 1974, which he has kindly permitted me to share. His report was based on twenty-minute interviews with five people in each of three groups chosen at random: those who completed the training; those who began but did not complete it; and those who did not sign up or participate in any manner. He chose the first ten from among the 160 inmates who signed up. (Of those, fifty-three completed the first training.)

Dr. Moss's informal conclusions were that the group which finished the training saw life in prison as more valuable and meaningful than the other two groups. He noted that "a subjective impression was that the [subjects in Group I] were more intelligent, open and generally able to express themselves. This could have influenced the semantic differential ratings; i.e., which came first, the est experience or the personality traits?" (In a subsequent report, he wrote: "Group I did not turn out to be more intelligent than the other two groups . . . they were somewhat better educated, more verbally expressive, tended to be in a greater number of inmate organizations, suffered less major reprimands, and showed greater self-control.")

Dr. Moss observed that those subjects who completed the est training were apparently more relaxed, more insightful, and more able to express themselves than those who had had no contact. He quotes them in his report:

I'm doing things the same as I was, but at least I know what I'm doing now . . . est is the solution to problems I've had for a long time. . . . It gives you a direction to solve problems. It helps me get along. . . . I found out things that help me that I should have known myself. est helps us see them better. . . . It's hard to put into words, but I feel easier about myself; who I am; why I do things. . . . I can really evaluate honestly why I do things I do. . . . I seem to have a better perception of myself and my surroundings . . . I can't explain it; I'm just accepting things as they are.

Dr. Moss notes, in passing, the "mystique connected with est" and that "no one seems to know why they [the prisoners] feel so strongly about it or how changes have occurred." He speculates that it might be the trainers' charisma.

In conclusion he says, "Regardless of the reasons, it is evident that est is a beneficial experience for those inmates who completed it."

The quote I like best comes from a recent prison grad: "I am now the guru of my whole unit. I got sixty guys following me around asking me questions about the way things are. They say to me, 'Hey, September, say it again what you said before,' and I say it again, and they say, 'Yeah, right on!' "

Jason

Jason is twenty-one, tall, lanky, with gentle blue eyes. I knew, through his parents, that he had been deeply depressed and that in the three years since he finished high school he had done little besides sleep and smoke grass. He recently got a job working with a golfer.

Going to est was really scary for me. When they kept telling me I was going to change my whole life I was scared of that. I thought they might do it.

They kept telling us that the room was a safe place but I didn't feel so safe there. I hated a lot of the people. I didn't want to go back the second day. Someone told me about a girl who had told him that she had cried the whole first night. That made me feel better, so I went back.

The only part I enjoyed was where everyone has to make a fool of themselves. I really liked seeing all those people who I was afraid of being fools.

The first month after the training I was in a panic, like I was being pushed into a corner. I thought I was going nuts. I went over and over what the trainer had said and my mind was throwing it up. Some nights I would go out behind the garage and sob. I couldn't understand why. After a month it stopped. I started thinking about what was really going on with me and the fear stopped. I stopped biting my nails and started playing the guitar. I began to get that I'm responsible for what happens to me.

I'm not a good salesman for est. But I started thinking intensely about what I wanted to do with my life. And I got a job. I'm learning all I can and I'm starting to take pride in doing a good job. I even started making my bed and keeping my room neat. I like the idea of cleanliness, which I never did before. My room was a mess. Now I'm thinking, "What can I do next to be better?"

My relationship with my family is a lot closer. I've always liked my father a lot but my mother and I didn't get along. Now it's great. I have a really nice family.

I used to blame everybody. Like I used to tell my mother, "You owe me something. You brought me into this world."

I get depressed for a couple of hours now and then and I move on to something else.

7

Tots, Teens, Grads, and Others

> *"I'm inventing new words and stuff. Like 'Nothing is impossible.'"*
>
> —*An eight-year-old graduate*

There's no such thing as being too old for est training—there was a man over seventy who trained with me. And if you're at least six years old, you're not too young. Although you can only *get it* in the training, est, like its participants, comes in many shapes and sizes.

Anyone who has graduated from the standard sixty-hour, $250 training can review the entire training after six months by sitting in on a training for just $10. (A special review training for graduates costs $35.) But if that's too much of an ordeal, or if graduates want to explore special areas or be involved with an ongoing program, there are the graduate seminars.

The graduate seminar program includes several seminar series, each consisting of from ten to twelve sessions and held weekday evenings. The cost is low—$27 to $30 a series—and is a bargain compared with therapy groups and college adult-education courses. (In fact, est says it loses money on these series when overhead and fixed costs are figured in.)

The purpose of the seminars is to support the movement created in the training and provide an environment where graduates can participate in their own and each other's growth. The seminars are not essential to experience the results of the training, but graduates are encouraged to take them. est states that "most graduates have chosen to participate in these programs after they have completed the training." The official estimate is that about 80 percent of a given class of graduates who live within seventy-five miles of a center register in graduate seminars.

While I could not attend all the available graduate seminars before I completed this book (there is no est center in Philadelphia), I did attend some in New York and intend to participate in others. I have found them valuable. What I experience is that I and others who keep attending est programs get clearer and expand what we got in the training.

The seminars currently being offered include: "Be Here Now," "What's So," "About Sex," "est and Life," "Self-Expression," and "The Body." The names of the seminars describe what they're about. Although each has a slightly different focus, the idea is the same: get off your point of view and see what's really going on with yourself. Some graduates have already taken all the seminars and are clamoring for more. I've been told that Werner is creating new ones to meet the demand.

My feeling about these seminars is very positive. From my professional viewpoint I feel it's important, and often essential, for any system that jolts the psyche to provide a follow-up for those who experience it. This is both to help the person integrate the experience and to ground him if he's frightened or disoriented by it. The encounter/sensitivity training/marathon one-shots of the sixties often failed to do this, an omission which was sometimes merely irresponsible and sometimes disastrous.

The est seminars provide environments, or "space," in which people who begin to expand in the training can continue to expand. It seems to me that this can have only a beneficial impact on both the individual and on society. est graduates are beginning to take a hard look at their own political, economic, and ecological irresponsibility in this country. Perhaps they will soon begin to ask for the same kind of self-responsibility from their leaders that they now expect from themselves.

In addition to the ongoing seminars, there are periodic courses, workshops, special guest speakers, and other programs. I have attended two large-scale events: "Something about Nothing" with Werner (held at Madison Square Garden's Felt Forum; capacity: 5,000) and "The First Special Graduate Event" (at Lincoln Center). These occasions draw enormous crowds with or without Werner. The thing they all have in common is a wonderful sense of camaraderie and of being a part of a community of people who are transforming their consciousnesses.

Werner once went on tour to introduce to est graduates Swami Muktananda, an Indian saint whose trip to the United States had been sponsored by The Foundation.* Friends of mine who attended the Muktananda event in New York were singularly disappointed with it. Among other things, although there was an interpreter, the swami didn't speak English.

And then there are the education workshops. Of the 14 percent of est graduates who are educators (teachers, counselors, administrators), 4,000 have responded to est's programs to assist them in adapting est to their work. The workshops provide a place for them to share with each other how they've used est professionally in teaching or learning and the results they've obtained. Out of this have come classroom trainings for children (the Watts training reportedly raised reading scores dramatically), in-service training credit for teachers, and courses based on the est experience. I might add that I've adapted some est techniques for use in my therapy practice and have found them valuable, as have a half dozen therapists I've talked with who have taken est.

The Communication Workshops are still another of est's programs. est describes them as including "principles and exercises designed to enable people to experience *true* communication (as distinguished from the plethora of words and symbols, that mass of explanation and argument, which is erroneously called communication). . . . When one achieves the condition of true

* est supports a foundation which makes grants for a wide range of conciousness-related activities.

communication, it results in harmony, diminishing effort, expanding understanding, and increasing affinity in one's relationships. In that area where there is true communication there is the experience of completion, love, and satisfaction."

Communication Workshops run for three nights and two days at a cost of $150. It is Werner's intention to support people whose job it is to communicate. Workshops have been conducted for a mixed bag of professional and special-interest groups, including psychotherapists, scientists, clergy, doctors, and nurses, among others. In addition, workshops have been held in Paris and London for est graduates and their friends who live or work there. In some of the workshops, participants need not be est graduates.

All these programs, incidentally, are highly publicized. est makes a big point about never advertising, but it is relentless in its efforts to invite graduates to bring newcomers to guest lectures and to attend graduate functions themselves. Almost no event passes without a pitch for at least one other event. And huge numbers of volunteers are continuously involved with mailings and phone calls to solicit attendance. At first, I found these tactics offensive, and I no longer do, as I take responsibility for *my* response to them.

I feel est's most interesting ventures are with youngsters—children and teen-agers. There are two teen programs, one a ten-day "live-in," which takes place in a secluded natural setting, and the other a standard training identical to the regular est training.

Werner, who has three teen-age children of his own, defines a teen-ager as "an adult who doesn't have his or her act together well enough to have it bought all the time." He talked about the teen-age training recently, describing it as "the single most important educational experience of my life. I discovered that no matter how old you are, you are still a teen-ager.

"The teen-age years are a period of struggle for identity," he says. "We are all still teen-agers because we are all still working hard to find an identity, which we think we need to prove that we exist. . . .

"In the teen training we do a breakthrough process, which is done as an activity until you lose control. The power releases when you lose control, when you are actually driven out of control. At that point [in the process], the trainees have the option of losing control or not, and the 1,000 teen-agers who have thus far been through the training all did."

"Once you lose control," he explained in his Madison Square Garden speech, "you find out what's true for you. And you find that out not by form, symbol, words. You cry, sob, you spill over, you see yourself. You see you *are,* not as a thought but as an experience."

In planning the live-in training, Werner created an intense space for this experience. Special emphasis is placed on diet, physical fitness, and open communication about drugs, sex, and related subjects. The brochure for this program says that teens "get to look at the patterned ways of being that they are afraid people will see about them. Once the pretenses are gone, they get to look at and communicate those things which they were using the pretenses to hide." When Werner is questioned about the teen-age live-in at graduate functions, his stock joke is, "We transform your teen-ager or we don't bring him back. So far they've all come back." The cost for all this is $750.

The est flier about this training includes part of a letter from a Washington, D.C., mother of two teen graduates. I was deeply moved by it (I, too, have two children). It says, in part, ". . . after the training, we were able to start off together at a point in our relationships that I would have felt lucky to have reached over a lifetime of trying. The training stripped away the patterns of our old, habitual transactions, unstuck us from our separate niches, rode right through the armor we'd set up to defend ourselves against one another . . . best of all, it totally erased all fear and anxiety regarding our future relationships together; there is simply no problem that we won't be able to handle."

Soon after I read this I met Sam, who is a living testimonial for the teen program. At sixteen, he is one of the most remarkable and together teen-agers I've ever met. Sam has long, shoulder-length hair, and looks like the kind that people used to label "hippie" and associate with rebellion, marijuana, and loose sex. He's a good-looking and bright product of an upper-middle-class environment. He took the live-in training two years ago because his father, a successful stockbroker and an est graduate, recommended it to him. Before he actually registered, his mother (divorced from his father) "checked it out" by taking the training herself.

"I had no idea how life worked before I did est," he told me. He didn't have any "really heavy problems" before the training —"just the usual teen-age stuff"—but he saw himself as "unaware."

The training was held in a mountain retreat a couple of hours outside San Francisco. "We got up at 6:30 in the morning, ran down a dirt road, and jumped into a mountain stream. There were sixty boys and girls, thirteen to eighteen. Werner was our trainer. I see him as totally powerful.

"I was skeptical before I went. I didn't think I needed it. And now . . . now I'm very clear about what it looks like I'm doing. And what I'm really doing. If you put your truths out there, you see that life works by telling the truth."

His clear brown eyes looked right at me, steady, calm, convincing. "When I get in an argument with my dad," he shared, "like I want the car and he says 'no,' I get clear on what's behind that trivia. I find out pretty fast if I'm playing power games with him and if I just want to be right.

"If I steal a handful of cookies and I'm confronted, I simply admit it. I accept total responsibility for what I do.

"My relationships with my friends are better. I had a silly fight with a friend recently. He was complaining because I was riding my bike in front of him . . . he didn't like his bike as well as mine. . . . He went on and on. Instead of fighting, I gave him the space to complain and be what he is.

"And my relationship with my parents is honest. When they get into fights through the mail or over the phone, I just stay out of the way. It's not my problem.

"Everything in the physical world is based on withholding tensions or problems hidden somewhere in the body," he explained, "and you get over it. And the upset goes.

"I think," he said solemnly, "that the way for me is not to look for happiness but to know why I'm upset. Then the happiness just comes. I think"—he laughed—"that I might even enjoy school this year. It will be the first time."

As much as *what* he said, the *way* he said it really impressed me. Sam was direct, specific, and honest. He didn't "play" to me. Nor was there any sense of superiority. He was spontaneous and very much his own person at an age when many adolescents are walking tragedies.

And then there's the children's training, perhaps the most remarkable of them all. Over 2,000 children have gone through it to date.

Any child between six and twelve, who lives at least six months of the year with a parent who has taken the training, is qualified to take it. The training is held for fifty children at a time, over four days on two weekends from 9:00 A.M. to 4:00 P.M. (they get it quicker, I'm told) and costs $150. My research indicates that the results are worth many times that modest investment of time and money.

est describes the children's training as "designed to enhance communication, participation, and responsibility. It is not psychological treatment or mental health therapy, and it is not necessarily for 'problem' children. The training provides the space for the children to better know and understand themselves and others."

Gladys Kassebaum, a school psychologist who is est's children's program consultant, has this to say about it: "Following the training, the children evidence greater assurance and calmness. They demonstrate increased directness in their communication with adults and peers and they indicate a sense of pleasure in their willingness to take responsibility for their behavior."

It sounded impressive. I wanted to find out more. I arranged to meet with a young man who periodically assists at children's trainings.

"The children bring in almost exactly the same problems and go through almost exactly the same procedures as the adults do," he told me. "They do a Danger Process. And, like the adults, they can leave the room to go to the bathroom only when the trainer permits it. However, the children's breaks are only two to four hours apart." He laughed. "But I think some of the kids have even better control than the parents." One difference he noted from the adult trainings was that the children were served lunch in the training room. His enthusiasm about what went on during these trainings, and the apparent results, was infectious. I wished I could have attended one myself.

They share about their parents a lot, he said, and it's O.K. to say things like "I can't stand my mother" and "I don't like my father." In response, the children's trainer, Phyllis Allen, will simply acknowledge their communication.

The assistant continued: "When someone gets out of line—that is, not keeping his agreement to be part of what's happening—then Phyllis has him take his chair out of line. When the child wants to rejoin the group, he tells Phyllis and she asks him to communicate that to the group.

"Phyllis then asks the child if he's willing to keep his agreements. 'I'm going to have the group applaud if they feel they're getting that you want to keep your agreement,' she tells him. And then she instructs the children not to clap if that's not what they feel from him.

"What's remarkable is that kids *get* instantly who's straight, who isn't, and who means to keep his agreement."

On the third morning the parents participate in the training for approximately one hour with their children. They share their experience of having their children in the training. Parents and children communicate about their relationship and look at their willingness to take responsibility for contributing to and supporting one another in a way that allows the relationship to work. There is also a post training in which the parents participate with their children and share their experience.

I heard all this first-hand from an eight-year-old est graduate and his parents, also est graduates, on my next trip to San Francisco.

Mason (not his real name) is a handsome, intelligent, clear-eyed child who was eager to share his experiences with me. He had taken the training a year earlier, when he was seven. "Now," he told me, "I sort of run things," which is est-ese for taking responsibility for his own life.

He began the interview with an overview. "Some parts of it weren't very good for me. I couldn't understand because I hadn't learned the words yet. Some I did know the words for, and that was more fun.

"I got that you listen and that if sometimes you don't like being there, you deal with it." He looked straight at me with his big blue eyes and I remember wondering fleetingly if this child wasn't an enlightened midget in disguise.

"I'm inventing new words and stuff," he went on. "Like 'Nothing is impossible.' That's one of my biggest ones. I didn't get that from the training, just sort of from my own mind."

He detoured to explain what a mind is. "Your mind is like a movie camera that shows 3,000 different movies all at the same time—word movies and picture movies—and it goes around. The pictures on the left side are what happened. The ones on the right side are what's going to happen. In the middle is what *is* happening. Like if someone says, 'Can you pour me a glass of milk?' first it goes on the what's-going-to-happen tape, then on the what's-happening tape, and then on the what-happened tape.

"The 'nothing is impossible' thing started when I thought of what it would be like to jump off a cliff and land in a tire or fall into a volcano and not get burned. And I thought, 'Well, that could happen because it hasn't happened.'

"But I don't think you should try it," he advised me. He went on to explain that he knows the real world works by agreement and that he separates that reality from the reality of his imagination. His grasp of incredibly sophisticated concepts was staggering to me. It reminded me that children already *know* what thousands of adults were coming to est to rediscover.

"Once I said to myself that the only thing that is impossible is to act like everything is impossible. The other thing is going through sixteen seconds of time and then going back and changing it. Now *that* is something you cannot do."

In the typed transcript of the interview tape there's a note inserted here by my typist. She wrote, "Is this kid for real?" I laughed. Later I told her that I felt he's not only "for real" but that he's more "for real" than almost any other child I know.

Mason's concept of time is that it exists by agreement and that the agreement states that time only moves forward and can't be changed.

He gave me an example of how this affects his own life. "I know that if something bad has happened, like when the atom bomb fell on Japan, it's not something I can care about. It's already happened and I can't take it back. If I could, I would care."

He related things of the past to things of the present with a "for instance." "If my Dad fell off a cliff and got beat up, I would say I half cared and half didn't." He thought about that for a minute and then added, "I guess I would take it back if I could." There was neither guilt nor remorse in that remark. He simply accepted that most of the time he cared about his father and sometimes he didn't.

Mason's parents were happy to share with me their experience since his training. They were grateful for it and spoke about their post-est relationship frankly and openly.

"One thing that's different now," his father told me, "is that I no longer keep the things from him that I used to because I thought he was too young to understand. I was totally wrong. There is nothing I can't talk about that he wouldn't be able to get, regardless of how complex I think it is.

"One day I was in a rotten mood and he said, 'Something is going on with you; is anything wrong?' I told him I was thinking about what had produced my bad mood, and he got it. I didn't know it was so easy. I thought kids didn't understand that kind of thing. After that, I stopped hiding myself from him."

He and his wife had sent Mason to the training because it had changed their own lives dramatically and they wanted him to have that experience. But they weren't quite prepared for the results.

"On the last day of Mason's training, when we went to pick him up, I naturally asked him what he got out of the training." This, from his mother. "He just looked at me calmly and said, 'I don't really need you.'

"I felt my head spin and my stomach turn over. I had learned long ago (a belief) that a child *shouldn't* feel that way about a parent. But now after est, I see that he may not need me or sometimes even want me. And that sometimes I don't need or want him. It is simply truth. But at that moment, I still couldn't handle my own child saying this to me.

"He could see how hurt I was. I turned my face away to hide my tears. When he went to bed that evening and I went in to kiss him good night, he was very loving and he said to me 'You're being the victim, Mom.'

"And suddenly I got that he was able to say this to me because he knew that I loved him. And he knew that I knew that he loved me. And that sometimes we both need each other very much and love each other and want each other. And sometimes we don't. And that he knew that I was being a sucker for plugging in to what he told me."

These parents were in touch with their emotional rackets, their games, their impositions on their child. He, in turn, saw not only through their rackets but also through his own. With that clarity there was space for all of them to be together. And to love each other.

If we multiply this kind of relationship many times over, we will get an entirely different notion of what being a family is all about. Once we can detach ourselves from the belief that children must love and need their parents all the time, and that parents must love and want their children always; once we accept that all feelings and experiences between parents and children are acceptable, then we can free ourselves and our children from guilt and dishonesty and allow ourselves simply to *be* together.

We can really love each other only if we can let each other be who we really are. I got that at est.

Janet

Janet at forty-eight is a beautiful bundle of energy. She is divorced and has five children ranging in age from fifteen to twenty-seven.

Talking about my est experience is like trying to share how I felt about my first trip to Rome with someone who never left Kansas. Or like telling how it was to have a baby.

I can't believe it. I can't believe the way I feel now. Just before my divorce in 1965, I had a nervous breakdown and I've been seeing a psychiatrist ever since then. He wasn't in favor of my going to est. He thinks my problems center around anger and he felt est might be a shocking way for me to get through to my anger. "Shocking" is his word. If I got those feelings out of my system, he told me, and if anything bad happened, it could cause another breakdown. He added that if the breakdown did occur, it wouldn't necessarily be unhealthy.*

I weighed what he said and decided to do it. I felt that if I had another breakdown because of feelings I couldn't express, I would benefit from it. I was going against him but it was *my* decision. I just said to myself, "O.K., my mother and father will freak out if I lose control, but my children are strong enough to take it. I'm doing it, anyway." Now I'm glad I did.

* est has a screening policy whereby anyone who has been hospitalized for psychiatric care or a mental disorder, or is in therapy now and not "winning," or who has been in therapy within six months of taking the training and not "winning," is recommended *not* to take the training. If the person does not accept est's recommendation, the enrollee must have a letter on professional letterhead from his therapist. The letter must state the following: (1) that the therapist approves of the person's taking the training; (2) that the therapist will be available to the enrollee during the training; (3) that the therapist will be available to the enrollee after the training.

The first day of the training was just dumb. I called the friend who had recommended it to me and he said that at the end of *his* first day he wanted to call the attorney general because it was such a rip-off.

On the second day I went back into my past and the feelings spilled out. I saw and felt myself as a child of about five. I felt unbelievable pain. I felt a ball in my left side as though I had just been hit. Then I saw myself as an uncertain, goody-goody little girl torn between my mother and father. I had never gotten anything like this kind of experience in therapy.

Now, since est, I can sit in my psychiatrist's office and be conscious of my body. When I get physical sensations, I know that what I'm saying is important. I might get a sharp pain in my stomach and, wow, I experience my anger. That's the anger I locked up in my body and never told my mother and father about.

Now I'm beginning to question what my psychiatrist is doing. I'm getting dissatisfied with him because I've gotten so much more out of est. I've been feeling a lot more. A lot of my pain about my breakdown and other things is coming out. And I can get angry at the children. The most important thing is that I'm not afraid now to get angry, right or wrong.

I only shared once in the training. I told people that my breakdown was a copout, that it was my way of escaping so I would have the support of a doctor. I said, maybe I didn't need that breakdown. Maybe I could have stayed strong and still gotten my divorce.

8

Werner and His Business

"I know that you know that I love you. What I
want you to know is that I know you love me."
—Werner Erhard

There's a photograph of Werner Erhard that appeared in print
which makes him look larger than life. I had bought this image.
When I finally got to meet him I was surprised to see that he is
only six feet tall. Lifesize. It was a little like finding out about
Santa Claus; I was both disappointed and relieved.

Unquestionably one of the most charismatic of contemporary
heroes—or anti-heroes, depending on which side you're coming
from—Werner has in just a few years in the limelight become
the focus of massive adoration, speculation, criticism, support,
and controversy. Everything he has done and does is a strong
statement. And a lot of it seems contradictory.

Witness:

On the one hand, he's the most influential person in the self-
improvement field today; he's been invited to conduct grand
rounds at the Langley Porter Neuropsychiatric Institute and
he's spoken at such distinguished places as the University of
California Medical Center, Stanford University, and the University of Munich. On the other hand, in a field where graduate degrees are an essential passport to success, his formal education
ended with high school.

On the one hand, his main theme is self-responsibility. On
the other, he walked out on a wife and four children, sixteen
years ago, to do his own thing.

On the one hand, he is regarded as the brilliant mastermind

and director of est. On the other, he is absolutely dedicated to minutiae (how to clean toilets; how to arrange chairs for a training).

On the one hand, he was born with a Jewish name (used until his mid-twenties). On the other, he adopted a name that sounds as though it comes direct from the Weimar Republic.

On the one hand, he appears the ultimate realist; to the marital status line on est's application form, he added LWS—living with someone. On the other, he appears a hopeless romantic; he expects forty million Americans to take the est training.

He makes terrific copy. He's a sinner and a saint, a supersalesman and a mystic, a preacher of pleasure and a workhorse, driven and peaceful, loving and demanding, and according to those who work closely with him, both sexy and neuter. He neither defends those parts of his life that don't fit into the American superman image nor does he hype his "good guy" stuff.

From my point of view, the main thing you have to *get* about Werner is that he's dramatically changing people's lives. "It's possible for you to walk out of here turned around 180 degrees," the trainers tell you, and it's true. It's tempting to knock who Werner is because of what he's doing, which is giving people what they want and making lots of money at it. It's also tempting to see him as a laugh on the psychological establishment with its rats and computers and unintelligible papers. As far as I'm concerned, that's not what Werner's about. He's a brilliant and effective superproduct of our times. And his work, I believe, is making a difference.

Werner Erhard was born Jack Rosenberg in Philadelphia on September 5, 1935. When he was five his family moved to Bala Cynwyd, my own Philadelphia suburb—a comfortable middle- and upper-middle-class environment with old Colonial houses and tree-lined streets. He spent one year at the same high school, Lower Merion, that my two children attended. He then transferred to another, from which he graduated in 1952. He may have hung out at the same local delicatessen which attracted my own teen-agers on spring afternoons.

I've had a chance to observe his parents on two occasions,

and my impression is that they are gracious, successful, and affluent people with a strong and positive sense of themselves.

After a thirteen-year period during which he had no contact with any of his family, Werner now has a close and loving relationship with all of them. Including his ex-wife, who has taken the est training.

I was extremely moved on one occasion when he shared his feelings about his parents. His mirror-deep blue eyes unwavering, he thanked his mother for teaching him about commitment (although, obviously, that seed took a long time to sprout), and he thanked his father for teaching him to be open and to love.

From high school, Werner had a quick succession of jobs: working in an employment agency; lugging beef in a meatpacking plant; and helping out in his father's restaurant.

He learned construction estimating and became a construction supervisor. For a short time, he worked in the automobile business as a salesman and as a sales manager. During this period, he also managed a business which sold medium-duty industrial equipment.

Shortly after he finished high school, he married his high school girl friend, Pat, and they subsequently had four children: Clare, Lynn, Jack, and Debbie.

In 1959, when he was twenty-four, he left his family "to avoid the responsibilities I had," he says honestly. He took off with Ellen, who later became his second wife and with whom he has had three children—Celeste, Adair, and St. John.

I thought of all this when I heard him talk recently about doing right and wrong things in life. "We make mistakes in life. When something is wrong, you have to acknowledge it's wrong. You also have to allow others to be wrong. Otherwise, you get stuck in being right." And later that same evening, "The soap opera you call your life is just a melodrama, evidence of the insane story you call your life."

When Jack left Philadelphia, he headed for St. Louis, the first stop in a long and arduous odyssey. En route, to avoid being traced by his family he changed his name. He read an article about physicist Werner Heisenberg and Ludwig Erhard, the German finance minister (later chancellor) and took his new name from a combination of theirs. He later said that "I had a very determined mother and an uncle who was a captain in the police department, so I wanted a name as far from John Paul Rosenberg as I could get."

(There has been a lot of flack about Werner's name change and the presumed disavowal of his Jewish heritage. He has never publicly denied this, perhaps out of respect for his father's family. In fact, he was baptized John Paul in the Episcopal church. His mother, Dorothy, is Episcopalian, and his father, Joe, was a Jew who converted to Christianity around the time of Werner's birth.)

With a new name, one suitcase, and "a life full of pretense and lies," Werner Hans Erhard disembarked in a new place and embarked on a new life.

He went to work in St. Louis as a registrar for a school that taught the operation of heavy construction equipment and sold used cars. He then headed to California, where he represented a correspondence school and enrolled students. Sometime afterward he went to Spokane, where he managed an office that sold Britannica's *Great Books.*

In 1963, Werner went to work for the Parents Cultural Institute, a division of *Parents' Magazine*. Recently, in response to a published attack on Werner's integrity, the man who was president of *Parents'* at the time of Werner's employment wrote about this period with high praise. In a letter which would make any mother proud, he said "Werner's very considerable reputation was based on his ability to develop personnel and train executives. His development courses were used by many other executives both inside P.M.C.I. and in other organizations as well. Werner's integrity, honesty and contribution to the well-being of the thousands of human beings he worked with earned him the respect and acknowledgment of the old and respected company for which he worked." Werner was vice president of this organization for the last three of the six years he was there.

He must have been a dynamite executive, given his charisma and his sensitivity to people. Fred Lehrman writes in *New Age*

Journal: "He seems to be a friend to everyone who wants to know him. I once went ice-skating with the est staff. Stumbling around on the ice for the first time in twenty years, I heard someone call my name. It was Werner. How the hell did he remember my name out of 30,000 graduates?"*

Werner left P.M.C.I. (which went out of business a year later), and became a division manager with the Grolier Society, Inc. A former associate and self-described friend of Werner's who worked with him at Grolier (and asked not to be identified) describes him as "supercool, aloof, and secretive. You never knew what he was thinking," he told me, "but he often said that he was going to build and make a fortune. I don't like the est organization," he added. "I went to several guest seminars but my ego wouldn't allow me to get into it." When I quoted all this to Werner, he laughed. "By that point I was long past wanting to make a fortune. I had already realized that money was no substitute for satisfaction."

Another view of Werner during his time at Grolier comes from his former boss, who was then the vice president. "Werner had a demonstrated ability to develop people's talents," he wrote. "He had a reputation for adding dignity and a sense of satisfaction to the lives of the people with whom he associated."

A friend of a friend sent me a copy of the Grolier house organ at the time Werner was there. It notes that the operation under his management was unique because, among other things, "The sales staff is comprised only of women. Recruitment is almost entirely in the hands of young enthusiastic women," it stated without comment, and then went on to note that "they consistently show up on the top ten producers list" and were "challenging their male counterparts." Even then he was top dog in his way, and his way was to do things in ways nobody else had.

During his employment with Grolier, Werner took the Mind Dynamics course and went on to study with its founder, Alexander Everett, finally becoming a part-time instructor. Accord-

* September 15, 1974.

ing to a former associate, "he worked with people to enable them to become more aware of themselves, even resorting to humiliation when necessary." Werner was offered a bigger job when the Holiday Magic people began to take over the active management of Mind Dynamics. Several months earlier he had had his experience "out of space and time" on which the est training was to be built. He declined the offer and left Mind Dynamics to start est.

Werner's wife, Ellen, was a very real support during the years he was developing est. She was a successful businesswoman in her own right, managing a natural vitamin and food supplement company which, Werner told me in her presence, he had started in order to give her an opportunity to experience her capability. She has since given the business to the employees and has gone on to assist Werner at est.

The motivation techniques Werner studied and taught with great success in business have also been translated for est use. Graphs and charts are maintained for all business functions, including statistics on how many people are enrolled in seminars and trainings. These sheets, which look like stock market analyses, are referred to and compared proudly; volunteers are apparently willing and happy to be "on the line" in their performances.

In contrast, Werner once told an interviewer that "motivation is kind of a joke that keeps people from finding out who they are. If they knew who they were, they wouldn't need motivation. They would be expressing themselves." He added that he doesn't think that he comes from motivation anymore. "I used to and taught others to. I was my own star pupil. Now it's almost like it just happens—it comes as an expression of my inner self—and the motives come afterward to explain it."

Werner is proud of his business background and credits it with being an important factor both in his enlightenment and as the school in which he learned much of what preceded est.

He says: "Business is such a beautiful place to [test disciplines]. If I had been at a university, I would only have dabbled in these things, because they would have been out of

my department. . . . Had I been in a religious order or any
church or monastery, I definitely could not have done any of
this. It would have been heresy. One place you are really allowed to do things like this is business, because business doesn't
care what you do as long as it isn't illegal and produces results.

"So when I told the boss I was going to use Zen with the
sales force, he said, 'Great, don't get any on the walls.' So I got
a chance to take my experience in Zen and translate it from the
usual setting to a new setting. . . . The thing that was really
beautiful about this translation of disciplines into business—you
really had to find out what the hell was trappings and drop it
fast. Also, translating demanded a deeper experience of the material to start with."

He went on to say that he was doing something at the time
called "executive development and motivation" and that his job
was to increase productivity, leadership, and executive ability.
A figure that Werner likes to use, and which is bandied around
a lot by est seminar leaders, is the 36,000 hours someone
figured out he spent in one-to-one and group sessions with people. "Six solid years, night and day, if you count it up," they report.

In another context, when talking about spirituality, he says,
"I spent thirteen years earning my living in the business jungle.
And that is where I learned about spirituality." He adds,
"That's all there is, there isn't anything but spirituality, which is
just another word for God, because God is everywhere."

While part of Werner's road to est was through his career,
the other part was through the various humanistic, psychological, and Eastern systems he pursued.

"I was a discipline freak," he says. "I did everything that I
could find and I found some stuff you wouldn't believe. I put
myself through as many different disciplines as I could find. I
either studied them or I practiced them or had people do them
to me or I learned to do them with people or whatever."

While he was in Spokane, he was involved with hypnosis,
motivation, yoga, mind science, and the study of brain function.

While working at Grolier, he took up Scientology, as well as Mind Dynamics. Because the Church of Scientology automatically expels members if they involve themselves in any other discipline, Werner was expelled when he started est.

At one time or another, he told me, he also got into Plato, Whitehead, Hubbard, Wittgenstein, Maslow, Sartre, Fromm, Heisenberg, Carnegie, Heidegger, Wiener, Watts, Von Neumann, Ram Dass, Napoleon Hill, Maxwell Maltz, William James, Rogers, Perls, Freud, Jung, Bateson, Silva, Skinner, Norman Vincent Peale, and Einstein. What he didn't actually participate in, he managed to study and read about. Although he hasn't talked about it, I would guess that he also was into some of the hallucinogens—LSD, mescaline, marijuana—that were popular in the sixties and that heavily influenced the consciousness movement of the seventies.

Werner says he got "the message" while driving south on California's 101. He had a direct experience of himself. He explained, "It meant that I no longer identified myself with my body or my personality or my past or my future or my situation or my circumstances or my feelings or my thoughts or my notion of myself or my image. . . . I have to tell you that I realized immediately that verbalizing it was irrelevant. What I considered relevant was being it.

"I didn't find out another new thing—I didn't add to my store of fact and information," he explained to me. "This experience transformed the quality of everything I knew—of my whole store of facts, memories, etc. Even the way I felt in my little finger was transformed. I didn't add any new facts—everything I knew, I knew now in a new way.

"It's like reading a book on bicycle riding. You know about balancing on a bicycle in one way. If you sit on the bicycle and fall off a couple of times you now know the same thing but in a new way. At that moment when it clicks and you can balance on the bicycle and actually ride it, you have not really learned anything new. You just know what you knew before, but you know it now in an entirely new way. That's analogous to what happened—it all clicked into place."

It was about eight years after his first experience of higher consciousness (which lasted three months and then was gone) that he experienced it again. In striving to regain that first experience, it continued to elude him.

"The secret," he found, "was that it [life] is already together, and what you have to experience is experiencing it being together. The striving to put it together is a denial of the truth that it is actually already together and further striving keeps you from getting it together. When I realized that, everything I'd already learned became transformed and I began from a whole new space.

"My enlightenment was perhaps somewhat unusual because I had an unusual disciplinary life up until that time. I lived in the toughest monastery in the universe, called the 'world,' only I did it as a monastic discipline.

"You know, most people fuck around with life. I did not fuck around with it. I did not handle life strategically. I handled it *all out*. I never got enlightened from doing it that way, incidentally. The discipline of working twenty-two, twenty-three hours a day and sleeping one, two, three, four hours a night and being always 'at it' for a period of perhaps thirteen years and less intensively for a long period before—that provided the 'stuff' to present the space for the experience of enlightenment. But that was not the enlightenment experience itself. est came out of my taking responsibility for and completing my own life."

est evolved out of Werner's own evolution. He says: "From all outward appearances, like most people, I was O.K. I had all the symbols: a wife who knew how to look and how to act, kids who were all right, and all the right material things. I had gotten good at pretending I was all right. I had enough of the things we all agree make a person O.K. But I didn't feel O.K. inside because I hadn't 'experienced' my O.K.'ness.

"After I got it, I began to see the truth behind what I'd done and studied. I realized: you can't learn truth from anyone; you've got to get truth from yourself.

"Of course I then discovered that it all had already been

said. Buddha had said it. Christ had said it. Socrates and Plato had said it. Gandhi had said it.

"When I realized the truth it was so stupidly simple; I couldn't believe I hadn't noticed it before. Finding what the truth actually is makes you humble."

What is the truth? "What is, is. What isn't, isn't." From there it was just one short step to the est training.

The product is consciousness—some people call it higher consciousness, expanded consciousness, deeper consciousness. Looking at the set-up—the numbers (250 people a clip at $250 per), the trappings (offices, houses, vehicles)—one can't help but conclude that est is giving people what they want. The product is a smashing consumer success.

Werner says he's not in it for the money. "I've worked on becoming a millionaire and I'm totally clear on how much bullshit that is. . . . Where I'm at with money is that I'm not attached to it. I don't shun it, I don't avoid it, and I don't run after it. I am responsible for it and it isn't what determines who I am or what I do."

However much he has or doesn't have (his salary is reported to be $48,000 a year), money certainly isn't a problem for him. He works and lives in two houses—an old Victorian town house which he restored in the Pacific Heights section of San Francisco, and a country house in Marin County.

The San Francisco house, exquisitely decorated with Oriental antiques and starkly simple furnishings, embodies the essence of est. "This house represents a lot of the est spirit," Werner says proudly. Fine food, good conversation, and hard work are all part of it. Thus, on one occasion you might be served dinner by a doctor or lawyer or restaurateur est graduate. On another you might be serving one of the same people. On still another you might be a guest at one of Werner's salons experiencing a physicist or mathematician discuss his work in relationship to consciousness. And on still another, although rare occasion, you might find yourself downstairs doing the hustle at a staff champagne party with the same people you worked with upstairs the night before.

Werner leases and pilots a small plane, a twin-engine Cessna 414. He wears impeccably tailored clothes. And he drives a Mercedes. The way he sums it all up is spelled out on his license plate: SO WUT.

But there's nothing offhand or flip about the way he has his business run.

At this writing, est has existed for four-and-a-half years. It now has offices in a dozen cities and runs trainings in all of these cities, as well as in schools and in prisons. In 1975, est grossed around $9,300,000 with a paid staff of about 230 and the assistance of 6,000 to 7,000 unpaid volunteers. Thus, est is clearly good business.

According to est's chief executive officer, Don Cox (Werner is listed in the est brochure simply as founder), est wasn't founded for profit. "Technically est is owned by a trust which operates it for the benefit of the public, to whom the value of est ultimately belongs," Don says.

Where, then, does the money go? Werner told me, "The purpose of est is to serve people, and to support those institutions of society that have as their purpose to serve people." As a result, est's philanthropic work has included six trainings, representing a contribution of well over $350,000; scholarships to clergy and to recently released convicts; and donations to hospitals and pediatric centers for work in child development.

During the last couple of years, est and the est graduates have supported a foundation that was founded by Werner Erhard. The Foundation makes grants for a wide range of activities in research, education, and public communication in various disciplines in the areas of consciousness, human potential, and the experience of the transformation of consciousness. During this period of time, The Foundation has made grants totaling $250,000.

An interesting aspect of the organization, which describes itself as an educational institution, is the way it emphasizes its contributions to education and its relationship to the educated. Werner, whose formal education never went beyond high school, has created an advisory board notable for the number and variety of higher degrees. In est's brochure, two pages out of fifteen of text describe "est in Education" and preface a listing of its programs and accomplishments with the proud statement that over 14 percent of its graduates—a total of almost 11,000—are educators.

Despite the good works est is doing, a lot of people distrust it because of its slick, big-business image. Mark Brewer summed up what I had been hearing among some skeptical colleagues in his put-down of est in *Psychology Today:*

"est is no ordinary California cult. It is a multimillion dollar corporation that has doubled in size each year and operates nationwide with the efficiency of a crack brigade. It boasts a President who taught at Harvard Business School and left the position of General Manager of the Coca-Cola Bottling Company of California to join Werner; it has been endorsed and even joined by prominent lawyers, doctors and psychologists; it has trained California schoolchildren under a Federal grant, and its Advisory Board is chaired by a former chancellor of the University of California Medical School, San Francisco."*

(I recently heard that a businessman from the Midwest who was planning to fly to New York to take the training cancelled his trip after he read the *Psychology Today* article. Like some others I've talked with, he apparently would prefer to entrust his psyche to a more modest, less successful savior.)

Others on the impressive est advisory board are Dr. Frank Berger, a psychiatrist who, among other things, discovered the tranquilizer meprobamate; the musician, John Denver; a total of eight physicians, three of whom are faculty members of the School of Medicine, University of California; two scientists, one an M.D. and one a Ph.D.; the dean emeritus of the University of California School of Nursing; a judge; an author and an editor; two attorneys; a community organizer; two educators; a

* August, 1975.

dentist; two businessmen; a social worker with a D.S.W.; a federal government official; and a local mayor.

The meticulousness with which Werner chose est's Advisory Board extends to every aspect of est's business. During the training, I was struck by how every conceivable possibility had been anticipated and prepared for. The printed materials are meticulous. The format for communications is meticulous. Even the way est staff members dress is meticulous.

More attention to the particular can be seen in the number and kind of communications emanating from est. Once you actually take the training, your mailbox will never again be empty. I get phone calls and monthly mailings. After I signed up for the training, I received two or three mailings and a couple of phone calls that reminded me that I had signed up, providing information to make certain that I got there.

No aspect of est's operation is left to chance or whim, least of all the staff. Those who work for Werner are carefully chosen and precisely trained. A San Francisco graduate who had once been invited to join the staff, and declined, told me, "He doesn't want people at headquarters who think they're doing him a favor. You've got to choose to be there, for no reason other than that you choose to be there."

The trainers fall into a very special category. As Werner's emissaries (I've heard them referred to, affectionately, as sub-gurus) the fourteen trainers are alter egos if not quite carbon copies and yet each has an individual personality and is his or her own person. They are rigorously trained over a long period. I understand that the main concentration of their apprenticeship is to learn to re-create "where Werner comes from" (with the use of videotape among other things) and for the trainer-trainee to get his or her own personality out of the way so the regular trainees can "be there" with themselves. That they all have the same air is, I suppose, a way of saying that the differences between them is irrelevant to the training. There are three women trainers, one of whom does the children's training. Word is that Werner is not a male chauvinist.

There are no specific standards for becoming a trainer—no

tests, no job descriptions, no applications for this position. Werner says that "many people come out of the training wanting to be a trainer. What I do is to set up an obstacle course and whoever gets through it is a trainer. The course is made up of anything they've been unwilling to give up, anything they're attached to, anything they need in order to survive. It's a huge sacrifice. What they really have to give up is their ego."

Trainer Randy McNamara used to travel with Werner and one of his jobs was to prepare Werner's tea during trainings. He says there is no difference between making tea and doing the training. Landon Carter began his job as trainer by being custodian of the San Francisco office. He says that he spent a lot of that time cleaning toilets; he, too, feels that doing the training is the same as doing menial work.

I watched trainer Tony Freedley conduct a Graduate Seminar Leaders Program one afternoon. The program gives graduates who have completed the Guest Seminar Leaders Program an opportunity to be trained to lead Graduate Seminars. He was putting the trainees through a mock seminar in which, one by one, they mounted the platform and delivered a portion of the seminar material. Tony was tough; he demanded nothing less than perfection from them.

I found the scene interesting. In addition to the trainees, there were est graduates who had come to participate and comment. (Several of them told me they came to anything est did as often as possible because the more they hung around est the clearer they got.) Tony put the trainees through their paces over and over. One was told, à la Dale Carnegie, to project his voice. Another was teased to lighten up his heavy approach. And another was chastised for not knowing his material perfectly. I felt that they got a sense of what it really is to communicate with people.

The trainers have gone through this kind of preparation—and more. The nine trainers whom I've seen in action have in common a kind of transparency, an objective quality, that transcends personality, judgments, and biases so that the only experience you get is your own right back again.

When I mentioned this to someone who had taken the training, she disagreed with me vehemently. "But they're always 'on,'" she said. "They're brilliant actors—stern and unbending sometimes, clowning and funny at others, beautiful, polished, clever. . . ." Exactly. What you experience from the trainers during the training is a duplication, out of their own experiences with Werner, of the training he created. Although they have a set format and a map of the ground to be covered and certain techniques and material to be presented, each particular training is shaped by the experience of the trainees in that training.

The trainer exists not as a teacher but as a catalyst, to *allow* experience. He never interprets what's happening, as would a therapist. He gets out of your way, leaving you alone with your resistance, your vomit, your headaches, your backaches, your hunger, thirst, or bursting bladder. He's there to hack away at your belief system. And to do that he has to be Dale Carnegie, John Barrymore, Jack Kennedy—*and* Werner Erhard—all rolled into a neat super-guru package.

In return for hard work and dedication—trainers work eighteen to twenty hours at a clip—est staff members get free medical examinations, insurance, and medical, dental, and chiropractic maintenance. And, of course, Werner's love.

One staff member described to me the value she received from being on staff: "I've experienced being supported by the others on staff and accepted as being O.K. just the way I am. I've begun to experience serving people, not coming from the position of need or help, but getting satisfaction just from serving. I've also experienced an increased amount of energy, getting things done that my mind says is impossible, and most of all, an enthusiasm for living."

est is all business and yet it is not business. The seeming contradiction arises because the staff at est really wants to be there. At staff meetings they share honestly what is on their minds without fear of repercussions and, according to Don Cox, president of est, "they aim at one hundred percent efficiency all the time and hit it frequently."

Don told me that "many high-powered executives who leave

other jobs and come to work for est hit bottom for a couple of months. They are just not accustomed to people really working and really getting the job done. What happens is they discover that they have barriers to operating at their full potential, and that's tough to look at."

Even the decor at est fits in with a total attention to detail and emphasis on beauty. The offices are elegantly simple and efficient. Don's office, decorated in shades of beige and with a few treasured art objects, reflects excellent and individual taste.

At the same time that he demands a total commitment, Werner also expects his staff to remain nonattached, both to him and to est. "You know," an insider told me, "if everybody dropped out of the seminar series that would be O.K. with him. Even if est were to fold that would be all right."

Here, again, was the theme of the so WUT license plate. It took me a while before I *got* it and recognized it as ancient wisdom from Himalayan caves and Japanese monasteries transplanted to the opulent and elegant San Francisco town house from which est is produced and directed.

Werner Erhard is an exceedingly complex man. Those who have summarily dismissed him as a con artist offering personal salvation to the tune of $250 have fallen into the trap of an easy, superficial explanation. It's an assumption based on conventional associations.

He is obviously brilliant and for some it may be more comfortable to label him charlatan than to look at what he has to say and what he's doing. Anyone who has experienced the training and who also has knowledge about the mind of man, and the traditions of philosophy, theology, and psychology, cannot fail to see how Werner has pulled them all together in a meaningful way that people who aren't philosophers, theologians, or psychologists can grasp.

It is easy, also, to write off what Werner is doing by seeing it merely as the sum of its parts: some basic Zen, a little Gestalt, a dash of Psychosynthesis, and some shrewd business management. That's like saying Picasso's work is merely the integration of all the brush techniques and stylistic devices ever created by all the great artists who came before him.

This point of view fails to recognize the mark of genius. Werner's genius becomes evident when you see that what a lot of great thinkers have been saying for centuries is what est is essentially saying, too. The difference is that est doesn't *say* it. Werner has developed a way for people to *experience* truth through their own experience.

With other teachers, you read what they have to say. With Werner you *get* it.

Aunt Anna and Uncle Harry

The following is an experience I had shortly after I completed the est training. The event was not hugely important. But it showed me how different things could be for me in all areas of my life.

I went with reluctance to pay a courtesy visit to my beloved Aunt Anna and Uncle Harry, who are eighty-three and ninety-one respectively. Although they have been an enormous and generally benign influence in my life, for the past year I had disliked going there because I was usually so uncomfortable during our visits. Uncle Harry is deaf, so it's almost impossible to talk with him. And Aunt Anna, once our opening platitudes are over, has nothing to say.

Driving to their apartment, I prepared myself for a miserable time. "They're not real to me anymore," I told myself. "They're among the living dead." I cried inside at what they had been—alive, vital, beautiful.

We greeted each other with hugs. From nowhere, suddenly, tears welled up in my eyes. I shared with them how much I loved them and how beautiful they both had been to me. I also told them how very much they had meant to me.

My uncle's face came alive. He said, "I didn't do anything special. I was just me and I cared for you."

I shared with my aunt my excitement about the publication of my latest book, *The Sexually Aggressive Woman*. I had not told her about it before, less out of concern for her reaction to the subject and the frankness with which I discussed it than for the fact that I had written on such an unintellectual subject. That was *my* evaluation.

My aunt asked me to put a copy in the mail to her when I got home. I definitely detected a gleam in her eye. And my uncle told me that he had, over many years, acquired a collection of great masterpieces on sex. Among them were a rare and beautiful copy of the Kamasutra and photographs taken at the famous Temple of Kondar.

Suddenly, we were all involved in an animated and fascinating conversation about, of all things, sex. This was because I had put away my preconceptions about what the visit would and should be. And allowed it to unfold spontaneously.

I had only *thought* my Aunt Anna and Uncle Harry were dead, which had almost deprived me of a beautiful experience of being with them.

9

Something About Nothing

"One creates from nothing.

"If you try to create from something you're just changing something.

"So in order to create something you first have to be able to create nothing."

— *Werner Erhard*

The street was filled with well-dressed, overwhelmingly white, predominantly young people. As I emerged from a cab into the cool August evening, I caught the excitement. The event that we all had come for was spelled out on the marquee. It said, simply, "Werner Erhard, est."

We were all est graduates who had come to hear Werner present "Something About Nothing." There were 5,000 of us who each had paid $4.50 in advance to fill every last seat of New York's Felt Forum. Werner had appeared at San Francisco's Cow Palace, before an audience of 11,000, and at the Los Angeles Sports Arena he talked to over 9,200, on the same topic. It was a major happening, a gathering of "the faithful" to be with their leader.

It seemed like an enormous family reunion. I ran into people from my training and we swapped "shares." People I didn't know introduced themselves and then launched into conversation like long-lost cousins. I remembered the first morning of my training when 250 "assholes" had stood around awkwardly —the only ones talking those couples or friends who had arrived together, the air heavy with anxiety, people looking isolated and alone. We had come a long way, judging from the intense interaction that evening.

At 7:00 P.M. sharp (est events start exactly on time) the doors of the Forum opened. I rushed for a seat close to the stage. I had heard that Werner was going to talk about his recent trip to Japan and his meetings with Zen masters. I had a special interest in Zen and was particularly interested in hearing what he had to say about it.

At that time, I had not yet met Werner. A friend had told me that "he makes you feel as though you are the whole world, as though nothing else exists." He had also been described to me as "contained," "complete," "dynamic," "beautiful," and "self-realized." Marcia Seligson, now a member of est's Advisory Board, described her first impression of him, in her *New Times* article, as "a slick, slightly oily salesman-type, too good-looking and funny, a man who reminded me of the arrogant Jewish princes I went to high school with, who then went to N.Y.U. School of Business, married girls named Bernice, and took over their father's clothing business."* I was eager to see for myself.

The air was alive with anticipation as we waited for the man who was to occupy the space defined by a lone stool under a white spotlight against a black backdrop. It was a setting for a torch singer, not a messiah, in an arena built for sports events, not enlightenment!

The lights dimmed promptly at 8:00 and Werner emerged from the wings. There were no tambourines or trumpets, no M.C., no benediction, no entourage, no props, no spectacle. Just Werner, looking much younger than his forty years, his skin and eyes incredibly clear, dressed in an impeccably tailored beige jacket, open-necked white shirt, and dark slacks. The audience rose and applauded. Werner had come to be with them.

He began quietly, undramatically. I found myself straining to listen to him. It took me a while to tune in to the way he was using words and the staccato rhythm of his speech.

"I do welcome you with all my heart," he said, "and

* October 18, 1974.

tell you that this really is my living room for tonight and I'm thrilled to be with you. As I said to Marcia [Marcia Martin, est staff member], I want to go to New York to *be* with the graduates and their guests. I said the whole point is really just to *be* there—not necessarily to *do* anything.

"My real purpose in being here," he explained, "is not for me to be but for you *and* me to be. . . . I'm here to create the space for you to be and I'm here to be in the space that you create for me to be. And that's the whole purpose, that's the whole point, and as you'll notice we've already achieved that so the night's a success as far as I'm concerned."

The audience responded to this introduction with enthusiastic applause. I was unmoved, waiting for something I considered "meaningful" to happen. Later I realized that one of my expectations was to be entertained. The circumstances of the evening —the theater, lots of people, an entrance fee—should produce entertainment, I thought.

"There really isn't anything to do," he said to my resistance. "I love you and I'm here to be with you. Besides which you will all get the chance to be with each other—and that's all that's going on.

"Sometimes people get very uncomfortable when all there is to do is nothing. See, in order to be, you don't have to do anything. It's terrific! There's nothing to *do!* It's really important to get clear about the fact that *you* don't need to *do* anything to *be.*"

The audience had settled in and was intensely focused on this magnetic and attractive (but not quite handsome) man with the body of a tennis player and the eyes of a prophet.

"In the ordinary course of events, we organize our lives to figure out what to *do* to get where we want to get. The point is, this is *it.* You got where you're going. Wherever you were heading, this is where you wound up. And that's how it is. You're *here.* Experience that you *are.* That's the purpose of this evening."

I felt as though he were talking directly to me as he continued on the theme that there was nothing for us to do that evening but sit back, relax, and just experience who we are. Because I wanted something—anything—to happen, I had a hard time relating to "nothing."

"I used to worry about what I was going to say in public before I got the training," he shared to laughter and applause. "I mean, what is the difference *what* I say tonight? It won't expand that you are one iota. And it won't contract that you are one iota.

"The entire universe comes out of the fact that you are," he explained. "Without you there wouldn't be any your-universe. What you call *the* universe is *your* universe. And there are a lot of your universes. The whole universe springs from *that you are*. You don't need to *do* anything, say anything, prove anything. It *is*. You don't have to work on it for it to be there. It comes from the fact that you are."

It seemed so simple. And so reassuring. To the thousands in the audience and the millions beyond the theater who had been raised on a diet of striving to please (Mommy, Daddy, teacher, boss), of trying to be better, richer, smarter, happier, this was heresy. But it was also manna. I processed his words and let them filter through all my "musts." It felt good.

He continued, enunciating the next words as though each were a universe unto itself. "The most fundamental experience you can have is *that*. There *is* no more fundamental experience than to experience that you are. From that experience, *all other experiences arise*."

He talked about all of our relatedness. "By the fact that you exist, my existence *is*. And by the fact that I exist, you exist. And we *are*. So we don't have to do anything to *be with* each other. We don't have to *make* our relationship work. We are related."

Then he spoke about his visit to Japan, where, he said, what he experienced was "being with life."

In a valley on the side of a mountain in an old monastery he met with a Zen master and seven monks. After a few polite interchanges they wanted to find out who he was and so they decided to test him. "It's customary," he told us.

"The Zen master showed me a very old tea bowl with strange symbols on it that had been used by many renowned Zen masters, and asked me, 'What is the most important part of this bowl?' If you say the wrong thing," Werner explained, "they go back to being polite and remote. I looked the bowl over slowly and answered, 'The space inside.'" It was the answer. They became friends.

He said that the Zen masters he met with were "blown away" by the fact that so many thousands of people in this country had taken the est training in only four years. He explained that a Zen master would consider that he had spread the word to vast numbers if he had trained a thousand monks in his own lifetime.

One of the things they had all talked about was the relationship of self experience to world experience. Contrary to our beliefs that those such as monks who live away from the world are aloof and removed, interested only in their own inner worlds, his new friends told him that experiencing the self takes you out into experiencing the world, which, in turn, takes you further into your experience of yourself.

Months later, in a letter to est graduates, Werner elaborated on this theme. "One of the ways you can recognize people who don't know who they are," Werner wrote, "is if they think that when you realize your self, it cuts you off from other people. Somebody who thinks that self-realization is the road to political irresponsibility has demonstrated an absence of experience of self. When you have experienced your self, you will know it because it will take you out into the world."

Werner then talked about est and its genesis. "est," he announced, "does not come *out* of the world. It doesn't try to give people what they *need*. It doesn't come from responding to people's deficiencies. est actually didn't come from any *place* or any *thing*. It comes *to* the world from nothing, from the fact that being just *is*, and there's nothing to be done about that."

(When I was working with this material weeks later it occurred to me that Werner's insistence on word precision often had the effect of making things more, rather than less, confusing to those not on his wavelength. I respect his work to revolutionize language and develop new modes of communication and agree that it is absolutely essential that we develop more effective ways to communicate. On the other hand, I think he defeats his purpose of communicating when his message doesn't get across to those who haven't yet achieved his clarity.)

Werner went on to speak of his doubts. He acknowledged that he has them and, "I let them be," he said, "and they let me be. They don't run me."

He related what he had once told a reporter in answer to a question about him as the source of est. "I *am* the source of est. I've created the opportunity for others to be responsible in their own lives, and they create the opportunity for me to be responsible. A source," he told us, "creates something from nothing." As the source of est it is his responsibility to create the space for the people in est to do their jobs.

I was becoming restless. I noticed that others were also. The material was familiar and not sufficiently dramatic to command my attention.

He returned to his discussion of where est came from, and told us, in answer, that it came from the experience that life doesn't work. "That's the most fundamental fact in est.

"Because people are always working at making it work, and getting those things which prove that life works, it doesn't." He leaned forward and readied us for a question. "If something actually worked, why would anybody be working so hard at making it work? See," he explained, "the work we do to make life work is an absolute statement that life does not work. If it worked, would you be working so hard to make it work?"

The audience giggled nervously. He was reaching us. His voice rose as he reminded us of what we all really knew. *"There's nothing you can do to make it work.*

"So I'll tell you what," he offered us. "If you stop trying to make life work, you'll have nothing to do. That's the first fundamental fact on which est is built. *Life doesn't work.* So stop trying. And, if you stop trying, you'll discover the second fundamental fact on which est is built. *You are.* That's what you discover when you do *nothing.*"

He chuckled. Some of us chuckled along with him in recognition of a truth.

"This is it," he announced. "This is *it.* This is all there is *right now.* No kidding."

I *got* that what he was saying was that all the effort and struggle and tight muscles of our lives came from trying to get our lives to work.

As I was digesting this and noticing my resistance to it, Werner spoke to what must have been a common experience. "The mind can't handle these facts," he reassured us. "And what happens in the training is that the mind is bypassed so the self can experience itself being."

The graduates applauded in recognition. As I looked around the auditorium I noticed that some people were deeply absorbed in Werner and others, like myself, were interested but not enthralled. When I was in the est office a few days later and discussed the evening with several people, I found a direct correlation between the depth of commitment to est and how people related to "Something About Nothing." A staff member told me that he had had a moment of enlightenment, "a complete experience of how it really is."

The evening then took an unexpected turn reminiscent of "This Is Your Life." Werner brought three of his seven children and his parents to the stage and introduced them to us. They were an attractive group, and it was obvious that he had great affection for them.

He told us that it had taken him a long time to grow up but that he had finally grown up—when he was almost forty. He then thanked his family for being who they were.

He then told us softly, "I don't have anything to teach anybody. I don't know anything that you don't know. I haven't got anything I can give you.

"People don't come to hear me talk because I'm great. They come to hear me talk because they're great. I'd really like you to get that *clearly.* The only purpose in being here is simply to realize your own worth. And somehow, if you and I just be, we get to participate in that worth."

I knew and accepted what he was saying but I felt, somehow, that I wanted more and was annoyed that I wasn't going to get it. He thanked us by asking us to consider ourselves thanked "for all the things I should thank you for" and then asked us to end the evening by getting in touch with "what your experience of my experience of you is."

Then he was gone and the lights came on. I had a fleeting sense that he hadn't yet been there and that the show was yet to begin. It was wishful thinking.

Exiting the theater and, again, on the street, I asked people to share their reactions, curious to know if I was alone with my feelings of boredom, disappointment, and confusion. Most of those I spoke with felt as I did. A few thought the evening had been wonderful.

A gray-haired man, who appeared to be about sixty and who was accompanied by his wife and two daughters, summed up what others had said to me. "I never saw Werner before and it was disappointing. And the training changed my life." He added, "I would have died a bitter man if it hadn't been for est."

A few days later I re-read my notes and thought about what had happened that evening. What I *got* was that Werner's talk, however obscure it might have seemed, was really what est was all about. It was the philosophy on which est was built.

I also *got* that Werner's Something About Nothing was the space he had given us to experience ourselves.

I felt that the discontent I and others had come away with that evening was because Werner had spoken to the space he thought the graduates were in, and that many of us were not in that space. Like me, they didn't want something about nothing. I felt that they wanted more obvious content—something about something.

Soon after this, another event was announced for graduates only, featuring trainers Ted Long and Laurel Scheaf. Ted, a former trial attorney who gave up his practice to become a trainer several years ago, was marvelous and theatrical. Laurel, a trainer-candidate relatively new to the public limelight, would add charm and sex appeal to the evening. It was to be another bona-fide Event.

Soon after Ted began, I realized that we were being given the pep talk people seemed to want, a review and a reinforcement of the salient parts of the training delivered in the punchy, riveting, straight-faced style est graduates are used to. The subject was "aliveness."

"There is nothing to do in life except live it," he said with a smile, "and you are qualified if you are living. Life as we *know* it is made up of concepts: 'I like it; I don't like it; I believe it; I don't believe it.' If you want to *experience* living, you have to get in touch with those body sensations, attitudes, emotions, points of view, and images from the past, which we're attached to—concepts which persist. That we get stuck at false cause is the issue. Adding more *things* to your life simply doesn't produce satisfaction. You only get *space* for yourself when things are all right the way they are."

I had heard all this before but, still, I related to it. Our belief systems are so deeply ingrained that if we don't notice them continuously we get stuck [fixated] with them. They are our point of view. In est talk we have to keep "coming off our point of view."

Just before the break there was the usual pitch for special programs for graduates. A few new ones had been added and we were reminded of those already in existence. I had my usual reaction when I heard this: I bristled. By now I was a confirmed est-er. And sometimes I still resisted what appeared to me to be the hard sell, which was standard at est events.

Ted came back to "consciousness" by turning to nature for an illustration: "When you plant a tree, you cultivate it, water it, support it, and it blossoms and bears fruit. If you immediately go and pick all the fruit and stop supporting the tree, then the tree dies." His point was that people who enjoy life concentrate their energies on supporting the tree of their life instead of focusing on gathering the fruit.

There was a process and then the closing message, an est classic: "Be responsible for the way it has turned out. If you can't, it runs you. There is nothing more to do."

The applause was enthusiastic. It was apparent that the audience had experienced something about something.

Bailey

Bailey is an exuberant and warm young man, about thirty, who was one of the early (1971) graduates of est. He did volunteer logistics for est for about a year. He now works for a California group that runs communication workshops.

Before est I used to blame the world and everyone I knew because my life wasn't working. Since est I know I'm the source of everything that happens to me. Like, it used to be that if it wasn't for my boss, I would work better hours or make more money. Now I see that wherever I am is where I created myself to be.

I had been totally dead for twenty-seven years. During the training I really felt I was a machine and it was very traumatic. Werner was talking about how we're all machines and my body suddenly began to feel different. My head got light and I felt like I was going to explode. I screamed out. Then I got up and said, "I am a machine!" It was a big release for me. At that moment I experienced who I was. Ever since then I've watched my life expand more and more.

I also got to see that my parents brought me up the way they thought it was best to bring up a child. That was all they knew. I had spent a lot of years making my father wrong because of my mother's hatred for him.

Last summer my father came to see me and I told him all the stuff I'd been carrying around since I was eight, when he and my mother were divorced. I told him, "Dad, you're really O.K. Whatever you want to do in your life is O.K. and I love you." Now we have a great relationship after twenty years.

My mother still carries all her negative feelings about Dad; she won't let go. She used to really upset me when she'd say I was just like my father. Now she can't pull that on me anymore, because I don't get sucked into her game. But I don't make her wrong for where she's at. It's her life and there's nothing I can do for her; she's totally responsible for it.

I really love her a lot. I love both my parents a lot. And I love my woman, who I live with.

Before est I never thought much about anything. I was just doing my thing, unaware, unconscious. I also handled relationships like my mother had. Like, since I'm perfect, why would a girl want to leave me? That idea would really murder every relationship.

I used to worry about death a lot, but not since est. Whatever happens, it's O.K. with me. I feel that the only thing that dies is the flesh; your being lives on. When I was a practicing Catholic, I was in fear most of my life. The nuns used to terrify me. I was caught between confessing my sins and going to hell.

From est I got that religious institutions are into survival, too, and that fear and guilt are their way of keeping you in line. I've read the Bible a lot, and now I see that the church totally misinterpreted what Jesus said. He kept telling everyone over and over that everybody was like he was: perfect. He was experiencing life, like Werner. He knew he was total source, living moment to moment, and was spontaneous.

Jesus is just another guru who happens to be popular here in Western civilization. I can't go into a church and praise Jesus. But I really got where he is coming from. He wants to let everybody know "I'm you." So my whole point of view about religion has been totally altered.

About est, I see that people really get attached to it. It becomes a place to hide for some of them, even for some of the staff.

I've taken all the graduate seminars and now it's all right for me not to go to est anymore. I've gotten what I needed.

I created est. I love it. I think the people there are fabulous because everyone wants to be there.

People expect est graduates to be perfect. They're really just the same as they always were except that now they notice what they're doing. People are also afraid of perfection. They're afraid that if they solve all their problems, there won't be any more.

There's no shortage of problems. And you can be perfect.

10

Where Werner Comes From: Grist for the Mill

"The truth is: You are."

—*Werner Erhard*

"It's all just a lot of mind-fucking."
—*A New York psychiatrist*

Werner says, ". . . understanding is the booby prize." He later amplified this to me, saying, "Understanding without experience is the booby prize in life." This chapter, nevertheless, is designed to give you some understanding of est. My intention is to convey a sense of where it comes from and the way it works. And I suggest that you cannot know est from what you are about to read.

To get the most out of what follows I recommend that you don't try to figure it all out. Maybe read it aloud or maybe just flip through it and read whatever catches your eye. If you don't make an *effort* to understand it, maybe you will.

At the gates to certain Eastern temples stand two fierce figures who represent guardians of the truth within; one represents confusion and the other, paradox. To find the truth, one must pass these guardians. est looks confusion and paradox squarely in the eye. And then moves straight through them.

The est training is a self-confrontation with one's own truth about one's self. Its ancestors, historically, include Zen, Buddhism, Taoism, physics, Vedanta, Yoga, Sufism, philosophy,

Christianity, Cybernetics, Scientology, psychology, Existentialism, semantics, and business.

Werner says, "While est can be interpreted as a compilation or distillation of a lot of disciplines, in fact, it isn't. But you aren't wrong to understand it in that way. Any point of view isn't wrong, as a point of view; and it's important to remember that any point of view *is* an interpretation—a way of understanding something."

I choose to see est as a creation, rather than a compilation. Werner has created est in the way a great artist creates a masterpiece, using techniques and materials that have been perfected over centuries to give his creation form.

The essence of the est technique, which both produces and *is* what you get (the medium is very much the message here), is to have people dis-identify from their minds, bodies, emotions, and problems, the story of their lives. This is done in the training by making it safe enough to "get off it" for long enough to step back and look at yourself instead of being forced to be yourself or defend yourself.

Every time your mind tries to justify a concept you have about who you are or what the truth is, it gets punctured by an insight presented by the trainer. This continuous pummeling of the chatter in your mind stops the noise long enough so you can *be* in silence. It is then you can *experience* truth.

The truth is: You are. For openers.

While each of us really knows that, the training allows people to know it with their total being—experientially. In an attempt to avoid discomfort, uncertainty, pain, or just plain boredom, we set up systems of behavior that keep us from being still enough to allow such things to come up. We smoke, make idle conversation and eat at that exact moment when, if we were to be still, the meaninglessness of our lives, the pain which we repress that only pops out as headaches and lower-back pain, the emotions which we suppress, would come to the surface and be experienced.

In the training people are given the opportunity to be with all those things which they have kept under the surface. As one by one these hidden things come up they seem an enormous burden on physical, mental, and emotional systems. Underneath the things people don't allow themselves to experience is the experience of their truth.

That is why we are asked to agree to sit in straight-backed chairs and not talk unless we are recognized by the trainer. That is why we agree to sit for up to seventeen hours at a stretch (relieved by one brief meal break and two or three briefer bathroom breaks). That is why we agree not to read, knit, smoke, eat, or engage in any of the usual diversions which take us away from ourselves. And that is why we agree to forgo tranquilizers, booze, grass, ups, downs, or the other things that make it easier on our heads—including aspirin for the almost inevitable headache. We agree simply to be there, without any of the props with which we usually avoid ourselves (TV, telephones, and toilets, among them).

We agree to abide by the rules of est for approximately sixty hours. The reason we do this for sixty hours is that Werner has discovered in his experience and observation of people during the training that this amount of time is "what works." By the end of the second weekend we *get* it.

As I experienced est, this is what you need to know (as opposed to what you experience) to get it.

The value of knowledge is determined by the *way* in which it is known. In other words, it's not only *what* you know, but *how* you know it, that determines how you *use* what you know.

All of our knowledge is held (or known) in a system which says that things work on a stimulus-response basis. When I communicate with you, whether verbally or nonverbally, you respond. (A nonresponse is a kind of response.) It's as if your computer buttons have been pushed, and whatever your response, it was programmed. While a computer may have a range of responses, we can only get from a computer the range of responses we programmed into it.

Werner says this about the way we function as human beings:

"We are stuck in the way we know—in a particular epis-

temology.* In common terms, we are stuck in our system of beliefs. Our whole language is based on this epistemology, on the
idea that what we believe is actually so; in fact what we believe
is based on a system of agreements which merely symbolize
what is so. Neither our system of knowing nor our language is
experiential. It only symbolizes our experience."

How can we talk about experience without a language to
describe it? We can't. Language, at best, only conveys something *about* experience.

The training introduces another way of knowing, a sort of direct exposure, or what Werner says is a natural knowing, where
real communication takes place. It is neither verbal nor nonver-
bal, since both of these come from and are perceived by the
stimulus-response system. This other way of knowing Werner
calls abstraction.

It's beyond believing. It's beyond thinking. It's beyond feeling. It's beyond sensing. It's even beyond doing. It's something
like the way Einstein must first have known about relativity, as
an abstraction beyond sensation, perception, imagination and
even beyond understanding. It's akin to that moment when it all
suddenly becomes clear after you've been working for days on a
problem. Without the addition of new facts, a clarity unfolds allowing you to see the facts in a novel way, which dissolves the
problem and reveals the truth.

QUESTION: How can you create something beyond knowing when all you know is knowing? ANSWER: By experiencing
it.

Experience, or what you and I normally call experience, is
the stuff that comes in from the outside. "But that," Werner
told me, "is part of what I call nonexperience.

"To explain that, let's oversimplify the process of life. Let's
enter the process at a point where something is happening to a
person. What happens is a memory is made and to the memory
we attach a system of concepts to explain it and make it reason-

---

* An epistemology is like the canvas we paint concepts on, or the container we use to hold ideas—epistemology is a way of knowing rather than
what we know.

able. Now the memory and the system of concepts begin to determine what happens. When what happens comes out of the memory and system of concepts, it is nonexperience.

"It's like a dog chasing his tail. Certain types of behavior are reinforced by what we believe, and what we believe is reinforced by that behavior, which strengthened belief more totally determines behavior, which behavior strengthens the belief, *ad infinitum*. We become automatons—with a slight difference. The difference is the ability to justify and explain the behavior. However, the behavior doesn't arise from the justification or the explanation. It comes out of those belief-behavior patterns and the explanations and justifications allow us to *pretend* we are free. My notion is that what happens in the training is that the individual is given an opportunity to create original experiences or to re-create original experiences instead of merely repeating concepts and beliefs—that is, imitating past experiences."

One way to get in touch with the abstraction from which experience comes is by "looking," really *being* with our body sensations, feelings, points of view, behaviors, considerations, and images from the past.

When we give up thinking, so-called logical inconsistencies become clearly compatible. A Zen koan asks, "What is the sound of one hand clapping?" Answer: The sound of one hand clapping. The answer is not, as it might appear, insignificant or irrelevant.

There are two realities: The ordinary reality, which Werner calls duality or illusion, and the genuine experiential reality, which Werner calls abstraction. What we call experience (sensation, feeling, emotion, mental strain, action, behavior, etc.) lies between our concepts and our abstractions. The truth starts out as an abstraction—experiential reality—and then becomes a felt, perceived phenomenon—what we usually mean when we use the word experience. *Then* the truth becomes a concept, memory, idea about what happened. Abstraction is all that is real to each of us *in our experience* and thus, Werner says, is the true reality. In order to live fully, we need to recognize and operate within both realities and keep one foot in each.

Although the true reality is our own experience, we still must function in the ordinary reality as though it were fully real. We do not have the option of jumping out a window and not falling. By choosing not to jump, we go along with ordinary reality, that is, the reality we agree on. Everything we don't know by experience, we know by agreement. This includes all of physical reality—that which has dimension, form, and exists in time.

This is what getting clear is all about: to accept life exactly the way we experience it to be and acknowledge that we are responsible for the way we experience it regardless of our beliefs, expectations or desires.

As Werner puts it: "Life is a ripoff when you expect to get what you want. Life works when you choose what you've got. Actually what you got is what you chose even if you don't know it. To move on, choose what you've got."

Once we choose what we've got, in other words, once we accept that *we* choose our experience, then it becomes impossible to blame *others*—parents, mate, boss—for our experience. And when we accept that whatever we're doing is O.K., that our choices are our own, then the conflict disappears. The prisoner who *got* that he chose to be where he is, ends up eliminating this conflict—and being able to be with his choice. It is resistance to what *is* that causes anguish. The only way to chip away at resistance is by getting into it, creating it, allowing it.

Conflict disappears when we experience something totally rather than storing it up in a matrix of concepts and beliefs. When we experience something so totally that there is no need to explain it, justify it, or understand it, it vanishes. Obviously, when it's completely experienced, the experience is complete. Nothing remains; it has disappeared. This is what est calls "experiencing it out."

When Dr. Dawes (see page 77) tells his young schizophrenic patient to force-feed his depression, he is saying, in effect: Experience your depression totally. Don't repress it or pretend to feel better or justify it with rationality. Don't ask for explanations or "How can I get rid of it?" Just let it be there. Experience it out.

Obviously something which is experienced completely disappears. Obviously, when a thing is complete, there's nothing more left of it—it disappears. There are notions within contemporary theoretical physics that tend to support this phenomenon.

When we are dissatisfied with a situation in our lives, and we try to change it, solve it, fix it, *do* something about it, we end up with a modified dissatisfaction. On the other hand, when we take complete responsibility for our dissatisfaction and experience it, it experiences out. Then and only then can we move on. In the training, people are given the space to both create original experiences, and to complete experiences they've been "repeating."

Taking responsibility is being cause, not effect. If you feel that no one ever listens to you and you want to be heard, you have a choice: You can find reasons, which might go something like, "My mother never listens to me." Or you can take responsibility for not being heard, in which case you have created the space to be heard. What happens next is you are heard.

When we put responsibility or blame or fault for a situation on someone or something else—that is, when we attribute *cause* to that other person or situation, we become the *effect* of that person or situation. As long as we continue to do that, we can never be in control of our own lives. What we create, instead, is our own variation of not wanting our mother to understand, or anyone to care, or anyone to listen.

Werner says, "If you keep saying it the way it really is, eventually your word is law in the universe."

We are the source of our own experience. All that we each experience in our lives emanates from ourselves. No one else makes us experience anything unless we choose that experience. Every human being bears the responsibility for "sourcing" his own life. In this way, as source, each one of us is "God" in his universe.

Where and what we are: We are much more separate and alone than we think. There is aloneness even in the most intimate relationships. Each of our realities, from the moment of birth, is ours alone.

Both psychologists and mothers, in their concern to be nurturing and loving, often deny what existentialists have accepted —that human separateness is unavoidable.

Everyone begins life simply being. Then the mind develops. est's description of mind is hard to grasp, but here it is to ponder: "Mind is a linear arrangement of multisensory total records of successive moments of now."

The mind *is* pictures or records of events past. It predicts the recurrence of such events, and survives by being right about its predictions—by winning, by dominating, and, conversely, by avoiding being wrong, losing, and being dominated. It is often easier for the mind to focus on proving how right it is ("See, I can't do blah-blah because I never got enough blah-blah as a kid") than it is to accept that being right is simply one of the mind's ploys for survival—and then to move on.

The more energy invested in being right (or wrong*), the less energy there is for aliveness. The paradox is that while mind exists to protect our being, it actually prevents us from experiencing it.

Ego is the mind in operation. Werner says that "the people who are interested in Ego or Ego Strength or Ego Reduction or Ego whatever would be well off to be clear about what Ego is. Ego is the mind in operation under a specific circumstance where the mind thinks that the being *is* the mind. That is all Ego is, and the 500 books written in Western psychology about Ego are confusing and the 1,000 the Hindus have written are even more confusing."

Ego begins when the being considers itself to be its own point of view, Werner explains. "It thinks survival is maintaining that point of view. An ego, therefore, is a point of view attempting to cause its own survival. So its purpose is domination of everything and everybody from that point of view. Ego will sacrifice its own body just to be right. This is the actual source of illness."

When we are afraid of something, we become *more* of it. The

* Wrong is actually a version of right. If you're always wrong—you're right!

more important it is for us not to be greedy, the greedier we get to accumulate the symbols of not being greedy. The more we resist anything, the more we become what we're resisting. It's obvious that resistance to something is a strong relationship to it—perhaps stronger than attachment. When we are resisting we often don't notice that what we resist is limiting what we can be.

If we don't acknowledge we're assholes because somewhere in our belief systems we're hanging on to "it's bad to be an asshole," then we are really assholes. And it doesn't make any difference. An asshole is someone resisting being an asshole.

If it doesn't matter, why est? Since we lie to ourselves about our experiences, we end up feeling confused and unhappy. The defenses we create are simply the mind protecting itself—surviving against experiences which would challenge its point of view. We then look for something—therapy, success, marriage—anything to bolster our defenses.

The problem with some therapies is that the "experiences" they foster are often only meaningful within the confines of the therapy relationship. The truth imposed from a place of authority only succeeds in further hiding one's own truth. Our own truth can only be known by creating it and recreating it.

est says what it offers is an opportunity to create and recreate one's *own* experience and, in so doing, to "open an additional dimension of living to your awareness. The training is designed to transform the level at which you experience life so that living becomes a process of expanded satisfaction."

There are no promises, no specific goals. Trainees are told from the beginning to "take what you get." est takes them past the illusion of personality, past the mind, and on to transcend the mind by creating the space (the opportunity) for each person to experience himself or herself.

Werner says that est wants to accomplish what is already so. "You are. If that were understood totally," he explains, "then you could understand why it doesn't take twenty years. It happens like that [snaps fingers]. . . ."

Isn't this just another belief system? Some graduates use it that way for a while. Werner says, "est is a pretty strong experience and people who are looking to get attached to something will come and get attached for a while. They do that because they have a pattern of attachment—a need for attachment. Eventually even these people let go because the est experience allows people to become *un*attached from the need to be attached. They experience out their need for attachment."

The brilliance of est is that Werner after experiencing the truth was able to form a presentation of it that included what is known about the mind, and a number of points of view that had been held about it, in a unique and original way. He then developed a way for people to experience the truth beyond points of view. What I do in the pages that follow is take a brief look at est from within several of those points of view: the Freudian, semantical, and philosophical, among others.

Werner's position differs radically from that of Freud. Nevertheless, they have one important point they share: their understanding of traumas, or painful experiences which have been masked, repressed, and thus made unconscious.

In the Freudian model, primary process (the so-called id) consists of images of what's going on in the body, hunger, sex, thirst. What's happening here are "species-wide" patterns of survival.

Secondary process (or ego) is the relation of primary process to the "world." For Freud, ego is the way the fundamental instincts for survival are expressed by each individual in society. Ego reshapes our basic drives into a form more or less acceptable to society.

Ego is blinded when it is overpressured from below to gratify the basic needs of the organism. Primary processes (basic drives) intrude into ego* awareness, clouding it and rendering it unclear.

---

* Freud used the word "ego" to represent a mature, balanced adult attitude, rather than a subjective self-centered infantile preoccupation, as the term suggests in common usage.

Freud said that the most basic characteristics of the primary process are unawareness, nondiscrimination, and irrational association, in which reason does not exist. It is in this space that we began life. It is what our relationship to the world rests on. When we become upset or frightened, we react, out of primary process. The secondary process (mind or ego) gets lost or—more frequently—anxious.

Thus, Freud showed that ego is often driven to irrationality—and often disregards the reality it evolved to perceive, hiding the primary process beneath it.

What Freud describes as existing *underneath* the functioning of the mind is what Werner is able to assist people to consciously experience during the training.

Freud's original purpose in psychoanalysis was to create a situation in which a person could go beneath his mind (through free association) to "re-experience" early traumas and then, through that "re-experiencing," to have abreaction. In est, when a painful memory enters consciousness, it can be completely experienced. And est has demonstrated that such things completely experienced disappear.

In psychoanalysis and many other therapeutic modalities as commonly practiced today feelings are often used as a substitute for experience rather than as an entree to experience. The development of the humanistic psychologies was primarily an effort to get patients into feeling and beyond words. In the newer therapies, subjects talk less and experience more. In est, one goes yet a step further—back to the source. One goes to the abstractions (what est calls *true experience*) from which sensations, feelings, emotions, attitudes, mental states, behavior, thoughts, and concepts arise.

Among Western psychologists, Werner has probably been most influenced by Abraham Maslow (Self-Actualization) and Fritz Perls (Gestalt therapy). Maslow, to whom Werner pays tribute during the training, focused on healthy people and healthy needs, rather than on the pathological. His idea of normalcy was "the highest excellence of which we are capable" which, he said, "is not an unattainable goal . . . rather it is actually within us, existent but hidden, as potentiality rather than as actuality."*

Maslow's theory recognized that every person has a hierarchy of needs. Only after a need with low priority is satisfied can one seek the gratification of a need with higher priority. First, obviously, are the physiological needs. Until a person has sufficient food, shelter, and safety he will not worry about psychological needs.

est has come into existence at a time in our society when many people have met their basic physiological and psychological needs and can now pay attention to satisfaction. The est trainees are, by and large, a successful group of people. I've met doctors, lawyers, a symphony conductor, business executives, artists, therapists, and scientists, all of whom would be classified in our society as "winning."

They are discovering that once their material wants have been satisfied, personal satisfaction comes next. The est maxim that life is three feet long and that a lot of us can now be concerned with that last quarter inch called satisfaction is why est is easily comprehended by people who are winning. And Werner acknowledges that satisfaction is not the primary concern of hungry people.

Fritz Perls' work is a brilliant application of a theory of perception to emotional functioning. He took Freud's principle of the unconscious and his own concern with the "here and now" and put them together to focus experiences for his patients. He demanded that his patients attend to all the aspects of their experiences, including the entire pattern or form. This he called the Gestalt. Closing the Gestalt, was, to him, simply getting the patient to re-experience all of his experiences. Unlike many of his students, he was an undisputed master at getting out of the way of his patients.

The est training is set up so that the trainer, like Gestalt, focuses (creates space for) the experience. The trainer is not the source of it. And the 250 participants, all sitting face for-

* Maslow, A. H., *Motivation and Personality* (New York: Harper & Row, 1954).

ward in identical, uncomfortable chairs, agree not to interact with each other so that they, too, know that they—not each other—create their experience. The trainee chooses to listen to the trainer or not, to other people sharing or not, and to experience his response as he wishes.

Another insight into the form of the training is the work of the late Roberto Assagioli, creator of Psychosynthesis (whom Werner visited in Italy in 1974, shortly before his death). This system employs techniques of imagery to release the person from the boundaries of words, so that he can experience seeing with the mind's eye.

est and semantics: About the time that Freud was developing the theory of the unconscious, a well-known writer named Alfred Korzybski was developing the theory of general semantics.

General semantics deals with our symbolic functions and the way in which words conceal experience. Korzybski was concerned with communication between people and, specifically, with the discrepancy between the way things are and the way we say they are.

The semanticists recognized that we can never describe our experience with total accuracy—our experience of, say, a tree, or a feeling, or of anything else. We can look at it and know it as a total experience, but we can talk about it *ad infinitum* without at all conveying the experience. The semanticists identified the various ways in which language functions to represent, but not reveal, our experiences. They saw that language may hinder rather than assist in re-creating experience.

What Werner does in the training is to create a space in which the trainee gets to re-experience his experience and to look at the language and concepts that he is using to describe that experience, *and to observe the difference between the two.* He doesn't just tell people that there is a difference; he gets them to know and experience the difference. And therein lies the power of the training, and its ability to transcend the important contribution of the semanticists.

Werner once said, "There are only two things in the world, semantics and nothing." Nothing, being the context of everything, represents the ultimate truth. And semantics, being the form of everything, represents the content, or all that *appears* to exist.

He realizes that language is inadequate even to report what is going on in this process of distinguishing language from experience. As he puts it, "There is something going on beyond the mind, where you have just being. The being discerns, it differentiates. But here's the trap: The mind works with symbols, it does not work with direct experience. So if you talk to a being and its mind about beingness, no matter what you say, you say it with your mind and the other person hears it with his mind. Therefore it's a lie."

est and Zen: Werner has observed: "Although the est training is not Zen, some features of the est training coincide with Zen teaching and practice. Of all the disciplines that I studied, practiced, and learned, Zen was the *essential* one. It was not so much an influence on me; rather, it created space. It allowed those things which were there to be there. It gave some form to my experience. And it built up in me the critical mass from which was kindled the experience which produced est. It is entirely appropriate for persons interested in est to also be interested in Zen." Werner adds, "The form of Zen training is totally different from the form of the est training. And we came from similar abstractions."

For the Zen adept, it is all-important not to go through life carrying around yesterday and tomorrow. A Zen saying is: When you are hungry, eat. When you are tired, sleep.

This seems so simple. Yet, how many people do this? Werner has said most of us are asleep when we're awake and awake when we're asleep.

est and God: Werner has said, "Belief in God is the greatest single barrier to God in the Universe; (it is) almost a total barrier to the experience of God. When you *think* you have experienced God, you haven't. Experiencing God is experiencing God, and that is true religion."

est has happened so rapidly that a lot of professionals—psychiatrists and psychologists—as yet don't even know that it exists. As I sought evaluations from among my colleagues I found that those who knew about it through friends or patients who had been through it were impressed with its results but were skeptical. Those professionals who are est graduates were universally positive about it.

Dr. Herbert Hamsher, professor of psychology at Temple University, a practicing psychotherapist, a published researcher, and an est graduate, has this to say about it:

"While Werner Erhard does not offer the est training as therapy—and it is not—it is one of the most powerful therapeutic experiences yet devised. The difference between the training and therapy is that it does not focus on or deal with specific problems or conflicts; it deals only with the difficulties of living experienced by everyone, although each in their individual way.

"est is designed to enhance one's capacity to experience oneself and for that purpose it is unassailable. It is sensitively and intelligently constructed with such insight and psychological sophistication that it can't not work. It is virtually impossible to participate in the training and not experience oneself in new ways and to greater depths than previously.

"My personal experience and my experience with friends, colleagues, and psychotherapy patients convinces me that the est experience is of universal value. The specific reactions and benefits are clearly distinctive to the individual; what is general is the opening up of the person in a way which promotes personal growth and encourages 'here and now' living and experiencing.

"Far from detracting from or substituting for psychotherapy, my experience is that est enhances therapeutic movement and potentiates the process of therapy."

Dr. Richard M. Dawes, a New Orleans psychiatrist and trained psychoanalyst who had been in traditional analysis for seven years and subsequently studied Gestalt and TA, says this about est:

"I have seen [est] work with myself, my patients, and my friends. . . . A colleague who does a group at a hospital where I have individual patients is amazed at the change in my patients [and] how they are breaking through their barriers. . . ."*

Werner says that est in no way replaces the need for therapy and that he offers est to the psychotherapeutic community as a support to therapy—as something which may assist the true purpose of all therapists, the well-being of their patients.

A well-known New York psychiatrist who has attended est workshops (and who asked not to be identified) told me that he believes est's effectiveness is based on dealing with the responsibility of the conscious and in bypassing the neurotic complexes people work through in the therapeutic processes. He feels that any movement that makes people responsible, as opposed to the irresponsibility implicit in work with the unconscious, and that brings this concept of self-responsibility to people who might not be reached in other ways, has value.

His criticism of est focuses largely on its representations. He feels that it claims (though est denies it makes any claims) to accomplish far more than it actually does, that its depth is minimal, and that it makes change and growth seem easy, which they are not. He also feels there's a dishonesty in its approach, which states, in effect, "We have it; we won't tell you what it is but come and get it anyway." Some professionals are more disturbed by this type of criticism than by what they feel is lacking in the content of the program itself.

Most criticisms of est come from one of four main points of view: (1) that it is fascistic, (2) that it is brainwashing, (3) that it is too abbreviated to have any long-term or significant effect, and (4) that it is narcissistic. Each of these criticisms has been made in a different context. What follows is a summation:

(1) While he was president of Esalen, Richard Farson

* Dr. Dawes' complete statement appears on pages 77–80.

strongly denounced est as a "totalitarian neo-Fascist, crypto-Nazi outfit." In an interview in *The Village Voice* he described it as "the next step in exaggeration of the things we did innocently and thought were good." Soon after he made these comments, he left Esalen.

When writing this book I contacted Farson to see if he wanted to stand by the statement he had made to *The Village Voice*. He said that that quote had been "misleading" and made the following statement: "My main concern about est comes from the fact that in any educational program, public schools included, people tend not to learn much about what is in the subject matter or content of the program but, at a deeper level, they learn the method by which the program is taught. That is why school children learn more about competition than about algebra, more about sitting still than about history, and more about obeying adult authority than about reading. These lessons are powerful because they are taught not by the *curriculum* but by the *ritual* of education. When people learn, as I believe they do in est, that it is acceptable, perhaps even necessary, to coerce, abuse, demean, incarcerate and exhaust people 'for their own good' we have a classic means/ends dilemma and, I'm afraid, the precondition for fascism."

It's quite true that the structure of the training is predetermined—that the data and processes emanate in a definitive manner from the trainer. My feeling about the so-called fascism, however, is that those parts of the training which have been criticized were deliberately developed to jolt people into a space from which they could then be open to self-experience. Fascism implies creed and victimization. The est training has no creed, and people have free choice to stay or to leave, to keep their agreements or break them, to respond to instructions or not, to create their own experience or to be angry at the tactics.

est says that the real fascism—the fascism of mechanical conditioned behavior, justified by explanations and protestations, and without the experience of satisfaction—is alive and well, ruling most of our lives. People who have experienced themselves—who know the truth directly—cannot be enslaved.

(2) The brainwashing charge has been stated most outspokenly by Mark Brewer in *Psychology Today* (August, 1975). Concluding an article which questions Werner's integrity and est's validity, he wrote: "Any citizen is free to spend money experiencing himself as a mechanical anus, and therefore discovering himself to be perfect. To each his own. However, I personally distrust any organization that transforms and uplifts thousands through the nihilism of a belief system that denies all other beliefs as bullshit. The use of brainwashing techniques, ostensibly to enhance people's lives, becomes bizarre when the outcome is to create unpaid salesmen. Smiling, they march out each week to share their brainwashed joys with friends, neighbors and coworkers. . . ."

Characteristically, est chose not to refute Brewer's charges, in a letter published in the December, 1975, issue of *Psychology Today*. But nine Ph.D.'s and M.D.'s, all est graduates, did respond. Ignoring all but the brainwashing issue (the rest was such clear mud-slinging), they wrote that "dehypnosis" and "deconditioning" were more accurate descriptions. They went on to say, "In the est training, people are offered an opportunity to look at and be more aware of the belief systems and automatic patterns of living which get in the way of their experience of living. Unlike brainwashing, which destroys belief [and substitutes another], the est training offers epistemological alternatives in which people can experience their experience rather than reacting automatically or through a system of beliefs. *Choice,* not brainwashing, is what the est training is about. We have found that there is nothing to believe in est.

"The central issues for us," they concluded, "are these: (1) Does the est training force or cause anyone, overtly or subtly, to believe anything? (2) Have we, as est graduates, found our experience of living enhanced by the training? Our answers are (1) No. (2) Yes." The authors of this brief and direct response are an impressive array of well-known professionals in the field.*

* Earl Babbie, Ph.D.: Professor of Sociology, University of Hawaii; Frank Berger, M.D., D.Sc.: Professor of Psychiatry, University of Louis-

When we spoke of this article Werner told me that he feels that mature, intelligent, and thoughtful studies about est, even those which are critical, are important. If est is true in people's experience, it can only be furthered by looking at all its possibilities and by encouraging sincere criticism. If est is not true in people's experience, no matter how many nice things are said about it, and no matter how many people believe in it, it will wither on the vine.

(3) An article in the July, 1975, issue of the *Journal of Humanistic Psychology* by Larry LeShan doesn't identify est by name but clearly is referring to est when it pokes fun at a guru who "promised all sorts of wonderful and permanent changes in your life if you attended two weekends with him or one of his students."

Although LeShan admits that he didn't try the "short method," he is skeptical of its claim of a quick enlightenment. "It tends to distort our entire view of the great work and quest that we are engaged in—of the gardening of ourselves and others. It leads to simplistic beliefs [and] inadequate conceptualizations . . . There is no easy way to get there. As a matter of fact, there is no place to get to. We are engaged in a process of becoming more and more at home with ourselves, each other and nature, not an attempt to arrive at a place. There is value in most of the methods we are exploring. Someday we will be more successful than we are now in putting the best from each

---

ville, School of Medicine; Ouide Bilon, Ph.D.: Workshop Institute of Living Learning, University of Maryland & Gestalt Institute, Washington, D.C.; James Bush, D.S.W.: Mental Health Educational Consultant, Martin Luther King, Jr. Hospital; Enoch Callaway, M.D.: Chief of Research, The Langley Porter Neuropsychiatric Institute & Professor of Psychiatry in Residence, School of Medicine, University of California, San Francisco; Byron A. Eliashof, M.D.: Psychiatrist, Associate Clinical Professor, University of Hawaii Medical School; Kermit L. Fode, Ph.D.: University of California, Los Angeles, Department of Psychology & Senior Psychologist, Ventura County (California) Mental Health Department; J. Herbert Hamsher, Ph.D.: Associate Professor, Clinical Psychology, Temple University, Philadelphia & Head, Research Committee, ITAA; Jack Sawyer, Ph.D.: Fellow, the Wright Institute, Berkeley & Visiting Scholar, University of California, Berkeley.

together. When we are, however, there is one thing I can promise you. It still won't be quick and easy."

He goes on: "Buddha worked on his own development his whole life and not he nor Jesus nor Socrates ever promised it would be easy. . . . Somehow it seems unlikely that the Lord of Compassion would have advised his disciples to give up their hard work and buy an alpha tuner."

LeShan's style is witty and convincing; I'd love to read what he might write *after* he took the training. In response to what he says, I'd like to point out that est makes no claims about offering people enlightenment. As I see it, what est proposes to do is to transform people's *ability* to *experience* living so problems clear up "just in the process of life itself." It is not preparation for sainthood. It is merely a beginning, an opening, from which people can move on to new places in their lives.

About his skepticism regarding the long-term results from such a short-term experience, I would like to say here that I, too, was skeptical about whether or not the est high lasted. I, like so many others, have had high moments after encounter groups, meditation, and other brief or extended mind expanding experiences. But these feelings were always short-lived.

My own experience with est, and that of the professionals and graduates I interviewed, is that most people continued to experience growth and change over a long period of time. In many cases, in fact, the experience seems to expand with time. Among those I spoke with were graduates of the earliest trainings in 1971, when est began.

Werner spoke to this recently when he described, before 6,200 graduates, a reunion of the first thousand or so graduates four years after they had taken the training.

"My experience of these people," he said, "was absolutely inspiring [because] I could see that est had literally disappeared into their lives. It had become a part of the fabric of their daily experience. They were not stuck with est jargon; they were communicating and they were sparkling, alive, beaming and happy. And when they share the training with people, they do so totally out of their experience of their lives working.

"You see," he explained, "the training was no longer an exterior event—something that had happened to them. It was not a set of rules to follow or something they had to remember. They weren't carrying est around in a basket. It was simply where they were coming from."

(4) The charge of "narcissism" against est—the deification of the isolated self—was spelled out by Peter Marin in *Harper's* magazine (October, 1975). Like LeShan, he did not take the training; however, his point concerning the isolated self is valuable and reflects the concern of others that the new therapies are "a retreat from the worlds of morality and history, an unembarrassed denial of human reciprocity and community."

In a long and comprehensive article representing this point of view, he comes down hardest on the assumption that "the new therapies provide their adherents with a way to avoid the demands of the world, to smother the tug of conscience." He is especially concerned that, because of "the unrealized shame of having failed the world and not knowing what to do about it," graduates of est (as well as of the other "new disciplines") will abdicate their social and political responsibilities toward each other and the rest of humanity.

Ironically, I happened to read this article the same day my mail contained a communication from est with information on how and where to register to vote. The letter from Werner that accompanied this said, in part, "The experience of self takes you out into the world to serve others. . . . It is your willingness to come out of your experience into the world, to be responsible for its condition, and to participate in life that is making this thing [est] work."

Werner spoke to this issue in a radio interview: "It is a fact that individual well-being contributes to societal well-being. . . . To weep for the world is to say that I didn't do it. And I *did* do it. . . . So I have a very large problem with this business about weeping for the world; I think that's nonsense. It belongs to me; I want to be responsible for it, rather than weep for it. I want to get up and do something about it."

My own feeling about the est training, alone or in combination with the graduate seminar programs, is that it is both incredibly effective and undeniably imperfect.

I feel that it errs, for example, in not offering body work and an opportunity to experience oneself energetically, despite its concern with body sensations. Exercise and breathing techniques are invaluable for expanding the experience of mind and body. Arica and most of the yogas incorporate body work in their disciplines. And such systems as bioenergetics very effectively work through blocks using a combination of conceptual, emotional, and physical technique. This omission seemed even more significant to me after I heard that Werner gets Rolfed frequently and provides free chiropractic care, and sometimes Rolfing, Feldenkreis, Alexander technique, and other body techniques for his staff, a clear recognition of the importance of a healthy physical body. A graduate seminar titled "The Body" is a step in the right direction but the lack of body work remains a missing link in the training.

I also feel that the training is very spiritual and I originally did not want to acknowledge that. Werner, who himself has pursued a number of spiritual disciplines, says, "The heart of est is spiritual people, really. . . . That's all there is, there isn't anything *but* spirituality, which is just another word for God, because God is everywhere."

Many people have deeply spiritual, mystical, or "peak experiences" during or soon after the training. A young woman minister from New Orleans told me, "For the first time in my life I know God, not from faith but directly." Others described to me "sudden lightness," a revelatory "whoosh," and "going through a tunnel to a white light." Werner shared with me a letter he had received from a nun graduate, which said in part: " 'The glory of God is now fully alive!' and it is thrilling to see and experience the impact you have in helping us to experience, discover, and realize all the potential we have."

Despite some minor objections, I feel overwhelmingly positive about the est experience both personally and professionally.

Only last week a friend of mine, an attractive and successful department store buyer, arrived at my home in tears about her life situation. "I've had three years of analysis with one of the best analysts in Philadelphia," she said, "and I understand everything that happened with my parents; how my mother was hostile to my father and how I was put down by both of them. But," she cried, "it doesn't make any difference. I haven't changed anything in my life and I still feel awful."

It was a familiar story to me. I had felt the same way through and after my own psychoanalytic therapy. All those endless, expensive hours of monologue had done nothing to lift the Charlie Brown cloud that forever hung over me. The analyst *can* create space for experience, but, unfortunately, many analysts and therapists I've encountered don't see self-experience as the goal of therapy.

In the est training, on the other hand, people have very dramatic and deep experiences. The type of experience differs for each person. Trainees experience to what Werner calls their "level of possibility." While a religious person might have a religious experience, another might experience love (many report rediscovering their love for parents they had emotionally, and sometimes physically, discarded), for another it might be a release of long pent-up feelings, for another it might be experiencing an ongoing problem such as loneliness or fear.

Many people don't experience any effect from the training until days, weeks, or months later. At the post-trainings I have attended, there are invariably some graduates who share that they have become free of migraine headaches, asthma, backaches, former husbands, nagging mothers-in-law, and a wide variety of problems. I was at first skeptical of these Lourdeslike miracles. Eventually, however, I realized that they were almost inevitable as people give up their pretenses and lies; they no longer need to hang on to the body ailments and destructive relationships that camouflage their truths, and they are free to move on.

Because est makes every effort to screen out those who might not be able to handle the training, the incidence of psychotic episodes is low. est statistics show that since the introduction of its screening process in 1973 breakdowns are lower than in the general population. est says, "If you have a hundred people and you send them to the grocery store, a certain percentage of them will have psychotic episodes and if you send a hundred people to est, a *smaller* percentage will have psychotic episodes." No official figures are provided but it is my sense, through the professional grapevine, that such occurrences are rare.

est's brochure about the training states that it is specifically pointed out to people before they take the training that if they feel they need therapy or psychological, psychiatric, or medical services, they should see a therapist, psychologist, psychiatrist, or physician, as appropriate.

Shortly after the training begins, the trainees are informed (warned would be more accurate) that they might experience every emotion possible, that the experience might be very difficult and painful, and that their tuition will be returned if they choose to go no further. est also makes available to the trainee's therapist the services of Robert Larzelere, M.D., manager of the est Well-Being Department, for additional information about the training.

The most definitive evaluation of est is being prepared with est's complete cooperation. Their "About est" brochure states that "studies of est graduates have been conducted by well-respected, independent researchers, including a survey of 1,400 est graduates headed by Dr. Robert Ornstein, a noted psychological researcher [his position and credits follow]. . . . The results of these studies are consistent with what thousands of graduates have reported about their experiences with est."

I called Dr. Ornstein to get a copy of the study, and I was told by his secretary that the study, although completed, was not ready for distribution. When I later spoke with him, he told me he was reluctant to issue it for the reasons he had outlined in a letter he sent to the participants of the study last June. In it he cautioned that "the study is not, strictly speaking, an outcome study. There were no control groups of nongraduates, and subjects were not surveyed both before and after taking the est training. The study is a preliminary, self-report, retrospective survey of est graduates, focusing on health and well-being changes." He also stated: "the study revealed no evidence that est harms anyone.

"This study does not demonstrate that people's health actually changes, but only that they say it does." Nevertheless, he continues, "the reported changes are strongly positive and the findings are powerful enough to warrant further research in any of the areas mentioned above. We are confident of the reliability and representativeness of the data because our response rates are high." Ornstein goes on to state that "Respondents reported strong, positive health changes since taking the est standard training, especially in the areas of psychological health and those illnesses with a large psychosomatic component. These appear to be sufficiently strong to justify controlled follow-up studies of particular physical and psychological variables."

Another study was done in 1972 by Behaviordyne, Inc., an independent psychological testing corporation, on personality changes in people three months after taking the training. Its general findings were that measurable changes in personality do occur as the result of the est training; that these changes continue to manifest themselves three months after the training has ended; that more changes were noted for the female participants than the male; and that "the psychological picture that emerges is that of a happier, psychologically sounder and more responsible person."

In conclusion, I think est's philosophy and techniques speak for themselves. Werner has created a system that encompasses and yet goes beyond the viable disciplines of every age and is proving effective for both the laymen and the professionals who have experienced it.

Felice

———◆———

Felice is twenty-five, thin and intense, with fiery
black eyes that immediately held me. She is
Hispanic-American and grew up in a poor section of Brooklyn. She works as a psychotherapist
in a mental institution.

I was afraid of everything. People, the dark, bugs, animals,
crowded rooms, open spaces. I knew I needed help—that's
why I went to est. I chose January because that's the time
of year I get suicidal. I knew I had to live.

Now, after est, I know I *don't* have to live. The intensity of
my desperation is gone. My desire to kill myself is gone.
Every time I feel suicidal I deal with my anger and it goes
away. I have come close to death and now I see how ridicu-
lous all that was. That simple.

If someone used to criticize me, I felt the whole world was
against me. If it got too bad, I'd think about killing myself.
That was my out.

Now I can take what people say and ask myself, "Is it
them or me?" If someone says to me, "Felice, you're doing
a lousy job," I ask them how. If they can't tell me, I laugh
and tell them it's probably their problem, not mine.

Now I can fight with my boss. He was in a lousy mood
one day. I asked him a question and he answered, "Why
don't you look that up?" I felt hurt. So I said to him, "I feel
hurt. You put me down." He laughed and apologized.

I'm also using est with my patients. One patient left the
unit without permission the other day. When she came back
she started cluttering up the situation with a lot of junk—
excuses, reasons, justifications. I wouldn't buy it. I told her

I didn't want to hear her racket. I insisted that she take responsibility for what she had done.

I felt incredibly strong. And I think she felt better because she had to be straight with me.

I'm not so afraid anymore . . . of anything.

11

The Future

"Here is where it is. Now is when it is. You are what it is."

—*Werner Erhard*

I heard the other day that est expects to train 50,000 people this coming year. That's a lot of people putting out a lot of money and effort to go through a lot of physical and emotional discomfort for the prize which is the est experience. Werner's intention to train forty million suddenly doesn't seem quite so preposterous.

At this writing, est has opened an office in Chicago, bringing to twelve the number of cities in which it is operating; has completed workshops in Europe; has 12,000 people enrolled to take trainings scheduled through the next four months; and gets an impressive attendance at the guest seminars held almost daily on the East and West coasts (one recent New York graduate brought twenty guests to her post-training). This, just four years after it got started in a small office above a restaurant in the girlie show section of San Francisco.

It appears that est can become as big as it chooses, and it is apparent that it is choosing to become big. At this point the momentum is so great that est could continue to grow without effort. The only barrier to its multiplying is the current limited number of trainers (14) and staff. Werner expects unqualified excellence from those who work for him. And apparently he's willing to delay est's expansion until the work can be done at the same level of excellence achieved thus far.

As est grows and increasingly reaches into the heartland of

America, will it make any difference? I think it will, and I think that difference will be a significant one.

est's impact will not necessarily come directly from est, alone. Trainer Stewart Emery left est in 1975 to form his own business. Like the other trainers, he is dynamic and aggressive and I have no doubt that his variations on the est theme will be successful. If he is anything like Freud's disciples—Jung, Adler, Horney, among others—he will undoubtedly add his own consciousness and creativity to the master's. And in est's long future, others will probably follow.

Adding to est's expansion will be the teachers, psychotherapists, and clergymen graduating from est and actively using it in their work, as well as all the other graduates whose work and influence put them among our power elite, trend-setters, and image-makers. (In my training alone, there were two physicians, more than a dozen therapists and social workers, teachers, artists, dancers, singers, journalists, actors, business executives, bankers, high-level public relations and advertising personnel, and a television news producer.) These are the people we look to for our models and who create our value systems. A surgeon relating to a patient and a copywriter promoting deodorant coming from their est experience may have far greater impact on the culture than the so-called average American.

Werner appears to be reaching influential men and women in this country very rapidly. In addition to the standard trainings, he offers a different type of est experience—the Communication Workshops. Because these workshops offer a way of breaking through the barriers to true communication, they draw large numbers of high-level people, among them doctors, management executives, university faculties, and professionals in the fields of medicine, education, and psychotherapy.

A graduate in training with the guest seminar leaders program said to me right after Werner spoke about training forty million people, "Can you imagine what the world out there would be like if forty million people stopped lying to themselves?" To that I add: and became (like est leaders) clear-eyed, clear-headed, open, direct, in the moment, and rid of all the mental (belief systems) and physical (aches and pains) baggage that gets in the way of aliveness? Incredible!

The main significance of est's work and impact, as I see it, is to assist large numbers of people in getting in touch with their own experience, which is what other New Age consciousness groups are doing. Until recently only the avant garde, and relatively isolated gurus, were exploring new ways of being. The enormous success of Transcendental Meditation has begun to change that; those who are practicing TM are in the vanguard of expanded consciousness.

Werner Erhard takes the consciousness movement an *important* step further.

What est does is alter people's experience of their belief systems, beginning with their experience of reality and ending with an experience of the self's potential to know and to be. Relating that to our daily human predicament, what it does is transform dissatisfaction, confusion, emotional pain, and physical distress into health, happiness, love, and full self-expression—what est calls "aliveness."

You might say that's what psychotherapy and religion have been trying to do all along. True, but there are millions who have never embraced, have rejected, or haven't changed as a result of, therapy and/or religion.

Although I see est creating a revolution in the practice of psychotherapy (and perhaps in education and religion as well) by transforming those involved, est's impact goes far beyond providing people with ways to deal with their personal problems. Its most far-reaching effect will undoubtedly come from the issue of responsibility, specifically the notions of self-responsibility and of being at the cause of our lives. This will be seen in *all* areas relating to the human condition—politics, economics, ecology, family relationships, war, peace, health, creativity, to name just a few.

We have seen in this book only a hint of what we may expect. If, after the training, prisoners in the maximum security ward of a federal penitentiary take full responsibility for their crimes, then it is conceivable that our increasing crime rate may actually be reversed.

If, after the training, children stop blaming their parents for the problems in their lives, then we can create a future where they learn, grow, and run their lives out of choice rather than coercion. It is not surprising that where trainings have been held in elementary schools, the schoolwork and leadership abilities of the graduates (aged 7-11) show an immediate expansion.

If after the trainings adults experience their body sensations, their feelings, and their aliveness for the first time in their lives, then we may create a future populated by awake, aware, and alive people instead of the mechanized automatons most of us still are.

If, after the training, men and women come to grips with their relationships and deal in honesty instead of subterfuge, and reality instead of belief, then perhaps divorce might decline, and millions of children be raised in a loving, accepting environment.

A colleague of mine who took the training with Landon Carter, a young, handsome, and dynamic graduate of Andover, Yale (where he was a football star), and Harvard Business School—a Kennedy type—had a flash of him running for office. Imagine a politician who was committed to keeping his agreements and who took responsibility for his actions!

It has long been a dream that mankind could be ethical and loving, as well as creative. I think that we are closer to that dream today than ever before.

Unquestionably est will continue to expand; the demand for what it provides is phenomenal and will probably increase. There is always the possibility, of course, it could get bogged down like other institutions in its forms and become removed from its experience. If Werner's intention persists, however, I feel the future holds great promise for est and all its graduates.

For myself, having been on a consciousness-expansion trip for twenty years, I find that I am closer to my tears and to my laughter, experiencing myself right here, right now, not so often thinking about the past or the future. I find that I have an added clarity in experiencing others. I am there with them, being with them, in a way I was not before.

Werner says, "When you have experienced yourself, you will know it because it will take you out into the world. Not into a cave. Not into a monastery. But out into the world. And the way you go into the world is with compassion. Being out in the world is compassion itself."

If all of us who have experienced est go into the world with compassion, and if we bring with us the awareness, the creative power—and the love—that we each have rediscovered within ourselves through est, then we will be a mighty force for a new way of being.

I know that with my heart. And I got it at est.

Dennis

Dennis, at twenty-seven, is an ebullient young
man with laughing blue eyes and curly hair.
He works as a travel agent in New York.

I'm a happy guy and I still have some things that bother me.

I don't think I ever noticed before what communication
was all about. I mean, really paying attention to someone
else. I listen now.

I know I am the center of my universe. When I operate
from stuff in the past, I'm not seeing what's happening right
now. Sure, I can still choose to react the way I used to. Or
I can be different.

Recently my Dad and I were together in the car and I
was driving. He began his stuff. "Listen, Dennis, you're driving too fast, turn here, do this, don't do that!" Throwing his
shit at me. It used to make me furious, but I either didn't say
anything or I let it go.

This time I took a look at what was happening. I saw that
this was my father's way of saying he loves me. He can't
come out and say that but he can tell me how to drive and
how to run my life. I can deal with it now. Maybe I'll talk to
him about it soon.

When you go through est, you learn that getting stuck on
something just keeps it from working. When you let go, it
can work.

I let go last week of wanting to travel, which was the
reason I wanted a job in a travel agency. I said to myself,
"OK, I won't travel." On Monday, my boss called me in
and told me that I was going to Italy to lead a group.

I've been in the job eight months and all this time I've been
stuck on traveling. When I got off it, it happened.

What I'm getting to look at now that's really important

for me is the way I relate to female bosses. I get furious at the women I work for at the slightest provocation.

The woman I'm working with now blew up at me the other day because I didn't leave a phone message on her desk. Usually I would freak out at something like that.

I saw that it wasn't the message she was especially angry at. She was just upset that day. But, still, I became nervous. I could feel my face start to twitch, my heart was pounding, my head was spinning. And I had a silly smile on my face. It is only since est that I get in touch with my body feelings when I'm upset.

My boss looked at me peculiarly and asked what I was laughing at. "I'm not laughing," I said. "I'm just smiling." She told me she thought I had a warped sense of humor. That was what really made me aware of my nervous smile and the silly contortions on my face.

I took responsibility for her reaction to me. Before est, I would have been stuck on that incident for days, running it through my mind over and over and letting it take over my life. Now I acknowledge to myself that it happened and that I might bring it up again. After the first day of looking at it from every possible angle, you know, rerunning every aspect of what happened, it simply disappeared.

Another thing. I had never, ever told my mother that I loved her. On Mother's Day, I called her and told her just that. I just said, "Mom, I love you." It felt terrific.

Shorthand: A Glossary

"I am willing for you to have space to share the way you got how you run your racket and I have considerations. . . ."

—*An est volunteer*

Werner is deeply concerned with communication. The training gives considerable space to it—what it is, what it isn't, the way to do it, the way not to do it, plus a lot of opportunities to actually communicate. The Communication Workshops were created to transform people's consciousness regarding communication. And the language of est was created as a tool to facilitate true communication.

Werner says, "Anything you can communicate about, you can be with—at choice." He explains est talk as "incredibly useful and actually important when you are describing something that can't be contained in a person's belief system. What it does is allow people to know that you're not describing what they think you're describing." Considering there's a lot that's new (to the West, if not to the East) in est, it's not surprising that Werner is reportedly working on a new dictionary because he feels the existing ones are inadequate.

What follows is a compilation of words and phrases—the est shorthand—used in the training and by graduates. They're in two categories—words you can use and words you can use but which get you in trouble.

I should note that Werner looked these definitions over and stated that they were inaccurate if understood as the definitions he intended.

I totally respect Werner's desire for perfection and at the same time I want to give the reader some sense of est's special use of words, as I experienced getting them and as I have used them in this manuscript.

So these definitions are mine, with a little help from my est graduate friends and colleagues.

A. Words you can use and what they mean:

acknowledge: A recognition of one person by another.

act: As in "getting your 'act' together"; your front to the world.

agreement: A mutual understanding or arrangement about which it's understood that you're going to do what you say you're going to do. est places importance on choosing to be responsible for keeping agreements. If you break an agreement with est, you are expected to look at what is in the space between you and fulfilling your agreement. An est maxim is "Your life works to the degree to which you keep your agreements." Also, agreement is that by which you know, for example, that it is dangerous to walk in front of a bus; the way you know the physical universe.

and: Used in est to avoid invidious contrast; replaces the word "but," which is hardly ever used in est (see **but,** section B).

asshole: What everyone is before he or she knows what is real and what isn't.

assist: Aid to another person, coming from the assumption that the other person is responsible and at cause. Contrasted in est to "help," which puts the recipient at effect (see **help,** section B).

barrier: What's between you and experiencing your own perfection; the something inside you that prevents you from seeing what's going on both inside and outside you.

belief: A nonexperiential way of knowing, which often prevents you from experiencing and thereby accepting what's so; a preconception, usually a misconception, that you once learned and which keeps you from seeing what's going on right now; used in the expression "belief system," which is a whole bunch of beliefs on a particular subject, such as "love," "success," "Mother."

buttons: As in "pushing your buttons," triggering automatic behavior; reacting in a predictable way to certain stimuli and, especially, to things that relate to deep feelings such as love, anger, happiness, sadness. (Think, for example, of when and why you smile.) An unwitting response, accompanied by "reasons" that are actually rationalizations.

cause: Being "at the *cause*" of your experience is the direct opposite of being "at its *effect*"; to create your life, to make it happen consciously by commission rather than omission: if we are the cause of our lives, then we create our own reality and cannot be at its effect (victimized, powerless). A concept which, once experienced, gives people incredible power over their own lives.

chatter: As in "the ceaseless chatter of your mind"; means the voices that direct your life from such nonexperiential knowledge as beliefs, which impose judgments and decisions—"considerations"—on things and which distort or put up barriers to experience.

clear: As in getting clear, clarifying an issue; removing the debris that prevents you from seeing something cleanly and sharply; to free from doubt, restriction, and obstruction; cloudless. Closely related to "belief systems," which are what often prevent people from *getting clear*.

considerations: A person's value system; judgments, decisions, reasons, opinions; barriers to truth because they get in the way of seeing what's really happening; a part of one's experience, which is to be acknowledged before one chooses but which is not *why* one chooses; things people use to be right or to justify their behavior.

effect: As in "at the effect of"; the consequences or outcome of cause; when one is at the effect of life, one cannot cause it and therefore feels powerless and victimized. One can move from being at the effect to being at the cause by choosing to choose one's experience.

experience: What est is all about; the source of reality.

fabulous: An est acknowledgment of communication (est synonyms are: great, thank you, marvelous, for sure, very nice); has no relationship to quality of communication.

get, got: Means that someone realizes the meaning or significance of a communication or experience; a revelation; to Heinlein fans: "grok."

intention: Directly related to getting what you want; you achieve your goals to the extent that you're clear about your intention; the essence of communication.

love: A willingness for the other to be as he or she is and as he or she is not; in est, bears little relationship to the American concept (as portrayed in the likes of *Love Story*); a function of communication (contrary to popular notion, love is strangled by need).

mind: "A linear arrangement of multisensory total records of successive moments of now"; what we consider ourselves to be—the purpose of which is survival.

observation: The only way to know, besides "natural knowing"; opposed to belief.

on purpose: Going about your business (job, life, etc.) with intention and with your eye on the goal.

point of view: The stuff that makes you you; your thoughts, ideas, beliefs, concepts; in order to be able to choose you must come "off your point of view."

process: What everyone thinks is the secret magical ingredient of est but which is actually one of several; according to the brochure, "a method by which a person experiences and looks at, in an expanded state of consciousness and without judgment, what is actually so with regard to specific areas in his or her life, and one's fixed or unconscious attitudes about those areas. The intended results of doing a training process is a release to greater spontaneity." (In the training, you begin a process by closing your eyes and getting into your space, assisted by suggestions from the trainer. In life, a process is a learning experience.)

racket: As in running your racket, doing your same old "number"; the behavior that you always thought got you what you wanted before you noticed that it didn't; your old, and probably useless, patterns.

reality: est says that a test for reality is physicalness, i.e., dimension, form, and existence in time. That established, est then says that what we consider reality is illusion and the only thing that's really real is experience.

running your life: Whatever is controlling or dominating your life; used to describe events or behavior that you're feeling victimized by; for instance, "his fear of sex is running his life."

share: To communicate insights, realizations, or experiences.

source: Where it all comes from, which boils down to you; thus, you, me, he, she are all God by being God of each of our universes, which is really one universe.

space: According to Werner, " 'From here' is not space, it is distance. From here to the very edge of the universe is not space; it is distance. And what the physicists call space is actually distance. Space is that medium in which distance exists, actually where everything exists. Space is not measurable, it is only experienceable." To allow somebody space is to let the other person be, do, say what he wants freely and without imposing your own judgments.

truth: That which you experience. Werner says, "If you put the truth into the system in which you cradled the lie, the truth becomes a lie. A very simple way of saying the truth believed is a lie. If you go around telling the truth you are lying. The horrible part about it is that the truth is so darn believable, people believe it a lot."

unconscious: What we are most of the time, oblivious, "out to lunch," unaware; est gives people the "space" to wake up so they can look at their lives—and thus live them.

yama yama: Synonym for chatter, which is the automatic stuff going on in your brain most of the time.

B. Words you can use but which get you into trouble (no-no's) and what they mean:

believe: A lousy way to know something; a justification for what you're doing and thus irrelevant if not useless (see **belief,** section A). Trainees are exhorted not to "believe" est.

but: An archaic concept rarely, if ever, expressed in est circles and generally replaced by *and.*

change: An alteration of something in the physical universe; an alteration in form—as opposed to transubstantiation (which is what est is really all about).

help: To aid someone coming from the assumption that he or she is at effect, i.e., that he or she *needs* your aid (see **assist,** section A).

how: There's no way you can know *how* to do something; you can only know the way to do something (all of which is too complex to diagram here).

no: If it's used, I've never heard it. (It's incredible to me that sentences can be flawlessly and easily constructed to appear to say "yes" but actually say "no.")

reason: All the stuff we use to justify why we do things, which keeps us from feeling alive.

try: We avoid doing things in our lives by *trying* to do them instead of doing them, or leaving them alone.

understanding: The booby prize (the prize, of course, goes to experience—or getting it).

(John Denver dedicated this song to
Werner Erhard and everyone in est)

"Looking for Space"*
by John Denver

On the road of experience
I'm trying to find my own way
Sometimes I wish that I could
    fly away

When I think that I'm moving
Suddenly things stand still
I'm afraid 'cause I think they
    always will

And I'm looking for space
And to find out who I am
And I'm looking to know
    and understand

It's a sweet sweet dream
Sometimes I'm almost there
Sometimes I fly like an eagle and
Sometimes I'm deep in despair

All alone in the universe
Sometimes that's how it seems
I get lost in the sadness and
    the screams

Then I look in the center
Suddenly everything's clear
I find myself in the sunshine and
    my dreams

And I'm looking for space
And to find out who I am
And I'm looking to know
   and understand

It's a sweet sweet dream
Sometimes I'm almost there
Sometimes I fly like an eagle and
Sometimes I'm deep in despair

On the road of experience
Join in the living day
If there's an answer
It's just that it's just that way

When you're looking for space
And to find out who you are
When you're looking to try and
   reach the stars

It's a sweet sweet dream
Sometimes I'm almost there
Sometimes I fly like an eagle and
Sometimes I'm deep in despair

NOTE

For further information about est, write to Erhard Seminars Training, 1750 Union Street, San Francisco, California 94123.